ART SINCE POP

Thames and Hudson · London

ACKNOWLEDGMENTS

My thanks to Rosetta Brooks, Barry Curtis, Michael Hazzledine, John Stezaker and Jack Wendler for their valuable comments.

Text filmset by Keyspools Ltd, Golborne, Lancs.
Litho origination by Paramount Litho Ltd, Wickford, Essex
Printed in Great Britain by Cox and Wyman Ltd,
London, Fakenham, and Reading

ISBN 0 500 41057 7

Delacroix once remarked that a skilful draughtsman should be capable of sketching a man falling from a building during the time it takes the man to get from the fifth storey to the ground. Similar instant reflexes are required by chroniclers of the immediate past. The following text is therefore a sketch outlining some of the broad tendencies of 'mainstream' Western art during the last eventful decade, in reference to the work of a selection of representative artists, but excluding those associated with Pop art and those whose reputations were established in the 1950s.

Reproductions of artworks are always to some extent misleading; and this is especially true in the case of much recent art, which by its very nature – processes, performances, concepts – cannot adequately be communicated via photographs; therefore I urge the reader interested in the art of his own time to see it for himself before he passes any final judgment on its merits.

Theory and practice:
Modernist painting in the 1960s

All the major art movements which flourished during the first half of the 1960s – Pop, Post-Painterly Abstraction, Optical and Minimal – manifested a cool, rational sensibility that was in marked contrast to the Existentialist *Angst* of Abstract Expressionism, the dominant style of the previous decade. In the 1950s critical attention had focused on the work of the so-called Action Painters – Jackson Pollock, Willem De Kooning, Franz Kline and others – Abstract Expressionists whose dramatic gestures and splashy brush-marks had encapsulated the act of creation, hence their canvases were regarded as records of events or processes. This kind of painterly abstraction had been devalued by second-rate imitators who had reduced its emotional style to a manneristic technique, and therefore the more perceptive of the younger artists felt that a detached, intellectual approach and tighter pictorial control were required. Jasper Johns' series of *Flag* paintings dating from 1955 set in motion the anti-Abstract Expressionist reaction, and two important exhibitions of American painting, 'Toward a New Abstraction' and 'Post-Painterly Abstraction', held in 1963 and 1964 respectively, confirmed that it was complete.

The 'New Abstraction' show featured the work of Frank Stella, Ellsworth Kelly, Kenneth Noland, Al Held and others. In his catalogue essay Ben Heller claimed that these artists shared a 'conceptual approach to painting': a prescient phrase. 'Post-Painterly Abstraction' was organized by the art critic Clement Greenberg and included paintings by Held, Kelly, Noland, Stella, Jules Olitski, Ray Parker, Gene Davis, Darby Bannard, Helen Frankenthaler, Edward Avedisian, Paul Feeley, Sam Francis and Friedel Dzubas. According to Greenberg, Post-Painterly Abstraction was characterized by 'linear clarity' and 'openness of design', qualities which reflected the influence of the less gestural painters of the Abstract Expressionist generation, Barnett Newman, Mark Rothko and Clyfford Still.

1, 2   Newman's work was not fully appreciated until the last decade of his life (1960–70), when the scale, clarity and immediacy of his majestic colour-field paintings deeply impressed younger painters and

4

sculptors. However, Newman differed sharply from his admirers in that he was no formalist: no matter how 'minimal' or 'abstract' his paintings may appear they are always suffused with content; in particular, with notions of the Sublime and with Jewish mysticism. Newman's art was, in Thomas B. Hess's words, 'private in subject matter, moral in its choices, subjective and tragic in mode', whereas the work of the younger artists was 'public, hedonist, objective and theatrical'.

Among the latter were three talented painters: Stella, Noland and Olitski. During the early 1960s their work became identified with the formalist critical dogma of Greenberg and his followers, especially the writings of Michael Fried. In his influential essay 'Modernist Painting' (1960), Greenberg argued that the arts were distinct from one another because each possessed certain unique characteristics that it was the function of the Modernist artist to isolate; in the case of painting by rejecting the non-pictorial – i.e. ways of depicting form more appropriate to sculpture. According to this theory the unique features of painting were flatness, shape of support, and properties of pigment (the greatest of these was flatness because it was the only condition not shared by any other art). Greenberg maintained that, by discarding the non-pictorial, painting achieved purity, established its separateness and guaranteed its standards of quality. Unlike the illusionistic art of the past, Modernist painting did not disguise its true nature by artifice; on the contrary, it made a positive virtue of its inherent constraints. Naturally enough, this doctrine of specialization has been attacked for its reductionism and has been called 'preventive aesthetics', because it tells the artist what he must and must not do.

Some commentators were surprised when Frank Stella, at the age of thirty-four, was accorded a retrospective exhibition at the Hayward Gallery, London in 1970. They failed to appreciate that given the pace of change operative in contemporary art any painter who manages to produce significant work for a decade earns his old-master status.

Stella's crucial decision in 1959 to adopt all-over, symmetrical designs was prompted by a desire to find an alternative to relational painting (works containing a hierarchy of forms and in which various parts of a composition are balanced against one another). Similarly he employed a uniform density of colour in order to negate illusionistic spatial recession. Stella cultivated flatness, in his early monochrome stripe paintings (1959–63), to the point where he virtually eliminated the 'figure on the field' effect. His now celebrated series of shaped canvases resulted from the need to achieve a structural consistency between depicted, internal patterning and the painting's literal, external profile.

An elaborate theory of 'deductive structure' was devised by Fried in response to Stella's shaped canvases and later extended to accommodate the work of Noland and Olitski. As the paintings became progressively simpler the theories became correspondingly more complex, until the works were in danger of being regarded as merely illustrations of a critic's theories. Consequently, new work by Stella has often been greeted with cries of 'weakness' from critics disappointed that he had not adhered to the party line laid down (in their imaginations) for his future development.

In the early 1960s the functional separation of theory and practice – the former being the province of critics, philosophers and art historians, the latter being the concern of artists – was still accepted without question. By mid-decade, however, certain artists (those associated with Minimalism) realized that making explicit the theoretical basis of their art was too important a matter to be left to non-artists, no matter how sensitive and sympathetic, and they began to annex the role of the critic. In the 1970s their successors have assumed total responsibility for elucidating the theory underlying their practice.

Inexorably, Stella's reductive programme led him into the cul-de-sac of Minimal art. Rather than opt for the third dimension as others did, he chose, from 1962 onwards, to relax his self-imposed austerity. Stripes of a single colour were superseded by multi-coloured and multi-tonal bands which immediately encouraged spatial readings. The polygonal paintings of 1966, with their eccentric outlines and distorted perspectives, and the protractor series of 1967–69, with their curved, interlaced bands, confirmed that illusion had been fully reinstated. Formalist critics acknowledged that absolute flatness in painting was impossible to achieve, and therefore illusion was permitted, provided that it remained 'exclusively visual', involving sensations of depth rather than suggestions of solid objects.

The work Stella has produced in the 1970s stretches the Modernist painting theory to its limits. In outline his recent canvases are extremely irregular, reflecting the internal complexity and spatial ambiguity of their interlocked forms and tilted planes. Since they are predominantly collages of variously textured materials, even the description 'painting' is inappropriate. Like much of Roy Lichtenstein's recent work, they echo the Art Deco of the 1920s (a style revived *ad nauseam* between 1966 and 1973). Within the limited ambition of colour abstraction, Stella's works are among the richest and most compelling of their kind.

Admirers of Noland's paintings describe them as 'handsome', 'lucid' and 'elegant'; those indifferent to their charm dismiss them as 'bland decoration'. Noland, a protégé of Greenberg in the 1950s, is twelve years older than Stella but achieved fame at the same time. With Morris Louis (died 1962), Gene Davis and others, Noland put Washington D.C. on the art map as the centre of a particular kind of abstract painting that emphasized colour.

In the early 1960s Noland exploited the 'one-shot' impact of simple geometric motifs – targets, star shapes, chevrons – and identified figure with ground by staining acrylic paint into unprimed canvas. Within the context of formalist art, all compositional changes assume a critical importance, and consequently every alteration in the placement of Noland's images tended to be hailed as a significant advance in the progress of Modernist painting. A series of elon-
13 gated, diamond-shaped canvases straddled by broad bands of colour, produced in 1966, were the closest Noland came to achieving that synchronization of literal and depicted shape which distinguishes Stella's early work.

Traditional pictures invite the eye to penetrate their interiors, and to oscillate between surface and illusory depth. In contrast, the much flatter images of Stella and Noland obliged the eye to skid laterally across the
12 surface. For example, Noland's long rectangular canvases (1967–69) are traversed horizontally by 'streamlined' bars of colour of various widths and hues, and evoke sensations of speed. Their huge, mural scale – derived from the 'big canvas' convention of Abstract Expressionism – engulfs the spectator's vision to left and right and makes the reading of the paintings a highly complex procedure.

Noland continues to explore the dialectical relationship between colour and structure (Greenberg categorized him as a 'colour painter', while Fried preferred to emphasize his structure), and also the dialogue between image and framing edge. In his recent
11 paintings illusionistic recession is suggested by unevenly stained fields of colour; this indeterminate, cloudy space is bisected by narrow strips in opaque pigment which interweave to form a tartan design (they might be described as 'lyrical Mondrians'). In his early paintings Noland placed his emblems in the exact centre of the canvas and left the periphery bare, but in his latest work the reverse is often the case:

the central area remains hollow, and the image – thin bands of colour – hovers near the edge of the canvas where it acts as a putative frame.

Critical opinion is sharply divided as to Olitski's stature as a painter. However, all agree that Olitski's paintings are more problematical than Stella's or Noland's because they avoid tidy solutions to formal issues; indeed, Olitski often sidesteps them altogether in order to wallow in painterliness and opticality (the Greenberg/Fried term for pictorial illusionism addressed to eyesight alone).

From 1965 onwards – the year in which Olitski began to apply paint with a spray gun – he gradually reduced the number of drawn marks, or separate areas of colour, which might be construed as structure or depicted shape. Thus many of his colossal canvases appear to be rectangles sliced out of an infinite, multi-coloured atmospheric haze (Olitski usually retains residual marks near the canvas edge to prevent the haze from drifting away). Many viewers cannot tolerate the nebulous insubstantiality of these paintings.

More recently, Olitski has begun to apply paint with squeegees and brushes to produce a richly variegated impasto which harks back to the encrusted paintings he created in the 1950s. Barbara Rose asserts that Olitski is now trying to 'redefine painting as simply surface'. No matter what ploys he adopts, Olitski never seems able to escape the tyranny imposed by his innate good taste.

Both Olitski and Ellsworth Kelly were accorded retrospectives in the United States during 1973. Kelly, the veteran Hard-Edge painter, did not really belong in Greenberg's Post-Painterly Abstraction category because he had been studying in Paris during the heyday of Abstract Expressionism and his work owed more to Matisse and Arp than to American artists. By using colours of equal saturation, and by extending shapes across the whole width of the canvas, Kelly strove in the late 1950s and early 1960s to preserve flatness and to prevent figure/ground readings. We know from his exquisite pencil drawings that his crisp abstract forms were ultimately derived from a study of nature. During the mid 1960s his geometry increased in severity, and he created a series of variously shaped canvases generally divided into two or three areas of vibrant colour. Later he abandoned such compartmentalized paintings and produced separate panels, each immaculately painted in a single hue, which he juxtaposed in various combinations. These works functioned solely in terms of colour, surface and format. In this way Kelly defeated pictoralism: he did not depict coloured rectangles, he literally presented them.

Olitski's emphatic surfaces and Kelly's colour panels are attempts to overcome the inherent illusionism of painting, and as such they are part of a general tendency in American painting of the 1970s – known as 'Minimal' or 'Opaque' painting – which emulates the literal character of Minimal sculpture of the mid 1960s (see p. 23).

Bombardment of the retina: Op art

In 1964 the international mode known as 'Op art' was 'discovered' by *Time* magazine, although it had been around for years. The vogue for Op art, and for Kinetic art (art involving moving parts, and therefore operating in time as well as space), was consolidated by a series of exhibitions held in 1965; perhaps the best known of these was 'The Responsive Eye' (New York), featuring Yaacov Agam, Josef Albers, Richard J. Anuszkiewicz, Max Bill, Julio le Parc, Heinz Mack, Francois Morellet, Larry Poons, Bridget Riley, Peter Sedgley, Jeffrey Steele, Günther Uecker, Victor Vasarely, Yvaral and many others. In the same year Vasarely, who had created proto-Op designs as early as 1932, won first prize at the São Paulo Biennale.

Many members of the art Establishment were embarrassed by the mass appeal of Op art: the critics, by-passed by the non-art magazines, found themselves, for once, behind public taste instead of ahead of it; haughtily they dismissed Op as 'mindless'. Certain of the Op artists were equally chagrined by the popularity of their art, especially when they saw their work ruthlessly exploited by the fashion, textile and advertising industries. The fact that Op lent itself to instant assimilation by commerce has been interpreted as proof of its shallowness. Whether this view is correct or not, there can be little doubt that the saturation coverage given to Op design contributed greatly to its rapid obsolescence as an art style.

The term 'optical' applied to paintings is obviously redundant, since all 'visual' art, by definition, addresses itself to the eye. However, what distinguishes Op from other forms of visual art is that it takes as its subject matter, and relies for its mode of operation on, certain phenomena of the visual system that are inherent in everyday perception but which generally pass unnoticed. Psychologists have devised a number of simple black and white patterns which stimulate these phenomena, and artists can therefore claim no credit for discovering these designs. Their achievement lies in their ability to harness highly unstable optical effects to provide unified aesthetic experiences.

Optical paintings can be divided into two main types: (1) works which flicker, pulsate and dazzle the eye; generally these consist of precisely delineated black/white designs that exploit the optical phenomena of figural grouping, apparent movement (both across the surface and in depth), after-images, and moiré patterns. Artists who have produced this type of 'hard-core' Op include Vasarely, Riley, Steele, Morellet and Reginald Neal; (2) Less violent works that present spatial conundrums; these paintings exploit the optical phenomena of figure/ground reversals and ambiguous figures. Artists who have produced this form of 'abstract illusion' or 'perverse perspective' are generally American and include Josef Albers, Larry Bell (his early work), Ron Davis, Charles Hinman and Neil Williams.

Op artists invoked the spectator's (involuntary) participation to a degree unprecedented in the history of art. Furthermore, the viewer often needed to move physically in front of the artwork to elicit its full range of effects. Environments intended to provide viewers with a total experience were designed by Jésus Raphaël Soto, and by the artists of the French Groupe de Recherche de l'Art Visuel (GRAV). Grandiose claims were made on behalf of 'spectator participation' and the supposed 'democracy' of Op art (an abstract art which the man in the street could appreciate) by artists associated with GRAV and the European 'New Tendency' movement. Subsequently 'participation' became the catchword of artists working in many different modes.

At first sight Op art and Post-Painterly Abstraction appear to have little in common; but both were preplanned and totally abstract, both excluded the artist's 'handwriting' and favoured Hard-Edge execution. As we have seen, illusions played an increasing part in the work of Stella and Noland; therefore it is not surprising that 'The Responsive Eye' exhibition featured the work of Stella, Noland, Gene Davis, Kelly and Feeley in addition to the more blatantly Op artists. The major differences between Op and Post-Painterly abstraction were Op's tendency to disrupt the flatness of the picture plane, its indifference to the issue of depicted versus literal shape, and the 'busy' quality of its compositions.

Undoubtedly the most accomplished English practitioner of Op art is Bridget Riley. A typical painting in her mature style contains an all-over black on white pattern formed by the repetition of a single geometric unit. During the process of composition Riley subjects the individual elements to various principles of transformation with the result that parts of the pattern become animated, are distorted by tensions or enlivened by rhythmical movements. In my view the most successful of these works are those which respect the flatness of the picture plane and whose designs remain confined within the limits of the can-

17 vas. For example, in *Disturbance* (1964), a force field of ovoid shapes is held parallel to the picture plane and rigidly contained within a square format, and thus a simulacrum of perpetual motion is achieved: the ovoid units are doomed to shuttle back and forth in flatland for ever.

Colour presents more difficulties to the Op artist

18 than does black and white. Since 1966 Riley has tackled this problem in a series of paintings containing colour stripes which are generally separated by intervals of white or grey paint. These pictures are closer in style to American colour abstraction than her previous work (indeed one critic expressed the opinion that transatlantic influences were the cause of an 'abrupt decline' in Riley's art). As one studies the bands of colour, simultaneous contrast enhances their effect, and retinal decay produces after-images which are irradiated onto the intervening stripes of white until the whole surface of the canvas shimmers with the ghostly presence of induced colour. It is no coincidence that Riley's use of colour relates to Seurat's: her early paintings (1959–60) were Neo-Impressionist landscapes.

While operating within such abstract polarities as fast/slow, static/active, push/pull, and warm/cool, Riley's intention has always been to realize emotional as well as visual energies: that is to create an art which transcends Op art.

The gifted American painter Larry Poons made his name as an Op artist, but his subsequent development illustrates the temporary nature of such a classification. From 1962 to 1967 his paintings were composed

13

of small discs, of various hues, scattered across uniform backgrounds. At first glance the discs seem randomly distributed, but then they link up to form 'dotted lines' which extend diagonally across the picture surface and beyond; finally one realizes that the discs depend upon a lattice-like infrastructure. As Poons' working drawings on graph-paper show, the positioning of the discs is based on a logical system but it is never applied with rigid determinism. The brightly coloured dots and ellipses appear to move in all directions, and the after-images which they generate accentuate their apparent movement. The 'orchestration' of these paintings, their ingenious blend of chance and order, has prompted some critics to employ musical analogies; it is significant that Poons first trained as a musician, and also that he acknowledges the influence of John Cage.

Since 1967 Poons' painting style has undergone drastic changes. These transformations have revealed that his temperament is essentially romantic. In 1968 he adopted a much looser mode of expression, utilizing painterly brushwork, unevenly stained colour-fields and an extended sweet/acidic palette. More recently he has poured onto his canvases quantities of earth-coloured acrylic pigment, mixed to the consistency of mud, and by drying the paint quickly has created a cracked, rind-like surface. These highly tactile paintings resemble parched river beds, lava flows or relief models of the Earth's terrain.

Poons' latest works reflect the revival of interest in the 'gestural' painting styles of the 1950s – Abstract Expressionism, *art informel* and matter painting – that occurred in the United States towards the end of the 1960s, and the widespread influence of Action Painting's process aesthetic.

No doubt Poons has antagonized some of his admirers by altering tack so rapidly, but whatever mode he adopts his work always has authority and verve.

Triumph of the third dimension

Conceptually the autonomy of painting and sculpture as separate media can easily be maintained, but in practice the two frequently merge: wall reliefs for example partake of both conventions. Moreover, the two art forms continuously interact, though at any one period in history one usually predominates; in twentieth-century art it has generally been painting. However, during the 1960s the relationship underwent a radical realignment. Painting aspired to the condition of sculpture, and sculpture aspired to that of painting; the outcome of this rivalry was that sculpture supplanted painting as the primary innovatory medium.

Throughout the decade critics announced that painting was in crisis, that it was exhausted, and, inevitably, that it was dead. How did this situation arise? Ironically, the crisis was precipitated by the attempts of certain painters to deny the illusionism of painting. For example, Stella's early works functioned as whole units; also their thick stretchers made them stand proud from the wall and stressed their three-dimensional objecthood. At this point the Modernist painter could either revert to pictorial illusion or switch to sculpture. A failure to make a clear choice would lead to hybrid inter-media forms that were anathema to the formalist critics because they contravened the 'purity of medium' dictum of Modernist theory.

In spite of difficulties attending such an enterprise, a bold attempt to extend painting into the third dimension, while still retaining its integrity as a medium, was made by the English artist Richard Smith. In the early 1960s he was identified with Pop art because of his interest in packaging and the off-register colour printing of advertising photography; however, his concern was with the *methods* of visual communication, not the *messages* they transmitted.

At that time his palette was, by choice, 'sweet and tender', and his brushwork soft and blurry (a mannerism he derived from Abstract Expressionism).

In 1963 he constructed the first of a series of rectangular wooden frameworks with projecting parts, over which canvas was tautly stretched. *Gift Wrap*, a typical example, contains the forms of two cigarette cartons which thrust diagonally out of the picture plane; their large size and 3D extensions mimic the huge scale and built-out structures employed by commercial billboard artists. Smith has explained that he was not trying to produce sculpture: his intention was to reverse the illusionistic process of painting (by which solid objects become flat images) and to achieve a unity between the image of a box and its representation, so he 'shaped the canvas to fit the image'. Thus his aims were essentially the same as Stella's.

Seen from a frontal position, Smith's 3D device worked well enough; but from other viewpoints the contradiction between the forward lurching of the projections and the flat picture plane became obvious. One solution to this problem was to build freestanding forms. In 1964 Smith fabricated a number of works shaped like buttresses which stood on the floor with their backs to the gallery walls; and in 1966 he made *Gazebo*, a completely free-standing structure. Another possible solution was to scale down the extensions, and this course Smith also adopted in 1966.

In the next few years Smith dropped any suggestion of representation; he applied his acrylic paint evenly, aligned his colour to the contours of the shaped canvas and, in such works as *Clairol Wall* (1967), divided the work into discrete units to permit a sequential variation of form. These changes brought his work into line with current American practice.

Smith was not alone in resorting to the third dimension: even such committed painters as Kelly and Olitski created sculptures during the 1960s in an

16

attempt to resolve formal problems that had arisen in their painting.

Meanwhile sculpture moved towards pictorialism when it abandoned the pedestal and spread itself across gallery floors. Eventually sculptors treated the floor space as a 'ground' against which their sculpture functioned as 'figures'. This trend, initiated by Anthony Caro, has since been exploited by artists as various as David Hall, Carl Plackman, Carl Andre, Barry Le Va, Richard Serra and Barry Flanagan; it is now a cliché. Another sign of pictorialism was the strident use of colour – especially by the British sculptors of the 'New Generation' group – that was intended to minimize the solidity and tactile quality of the sculptural form while maximizing its optical appeal.

The hardness of traditional sculpture was challenged by the Pop artist Claes Oldenburg in 1963 when he began to make objects from pliable materials; a vogue for 'soft sculpture' followed. Later in the decade artists such as Bruce Nauman, Robert Morris, Keith Sonnier and Barry Flanagan employed previously non-sculptural materials – felt, flax, flock, rope – and hung their works from walls (like paintings), or propped them against walls with sticks, in order to display their inherent floppiness to full advantage. (A popular slang maxim of the day was 'let it all hang out'.)

In turn these flaccid sculptures encouraged painters to diminish the objecthood of stretched canvases by removing the stretchers; for example Richard Tuttle employed pieces of irregularly shaped, dyed canvas which he tacked to the gallery wall or floor; Sam Gilliam draped loose bolts of canvas from various points along a wall or suspended them from various points on a ceiling. By elaborately staining his canvases with pigment Gilliam asserted their status as paintings; but by draping them like curtains he simultaneously suggested that they were sculpture.

17

Robert Morris (1931–). *Installation*, 1968. Felt pieces. Photo Leo Castelli Gallery.

The result was a contrived and uneasy mixture of
32 genres. Richard Smith's recent works, shown in London in 1973, reveal that he too has renounced the use of stretchers: now he links several separate pieces of canvas by means of struts and attaches the irregularly shaped membrane to the wall by a centrally placed plumb line; these paintings somewhat resemble kites or sails.

Minimal art, the dominant mode of the mid-1960s in America, was almost exclusively three-dimensional in form; but, paradoxically, it owed little to post-1945 sculptural traditions: rather it was developed in response to the impasse that painting had reached. Donald Judd, one of the chief exponents of Minimal art, explains in his essay 'Specific Objects' (1965) that his generation found the basic characteristics of painting – those vaunted by Greenberg – far too restricting, and that they resorted to the third dimension because of its unlimited potential, because it was 'real space' and therefore avoided 'the problem of illusionism'. Judd was reluctant to call the new objects 'sculpture' because he believed that sculpture, like painting, had become a 'set form'; hence his neutral description 'three-dimensional work'.

A crude guide as to whether a work counts as painting or sculpture is whether it is hung on a wall or displayed on the floor. Many of Judd's own works – those composed of a number of identical units – defeat this rule of thumb by being equally at home on wall or floor. The West Coast American artist John McCracken is noted for his impeccably finished *Planks* – oblongs of wood or fibreglass sprayed with layers of automobile lacquer – which he presents in galleries by standing them on the floor and leaning them against the wall. These works defy classification as either painting or sculpture; they seem to condense the two media into a single new convention.

Although sculpture triumphed in the internecine war between painting and sculpture, its victory was shortlived. The conflict revealed that both media were uncertain of their identities. Shortly afterwards, avant-garde artists rejected the priority of orthodox media and were prepared to employ any medium, or combination of media, capable of giving concrete expression to actions, processes or concepts.

Modernist sculpture in Britain

In Britain the ascendancy of sculpture over painting was demonstrated by two exhibitions held at the Whitechapel Gallery, namely Anthony Caro's one-man show (1963) and 'The New Generation' (1965). Although at one time an assistant of Henry Moore, Caro was inspired by American art, in particular by the welded metal sculpture of David Smith and the paintings of the New Abstractionists. In 1959 Caro visited the States and met Greenberg and Noland; later his work became sufficiently 'advanced' and 'Modernist' to merit praise from Greenberg and Fried.

Caro established his reputation by creating a type of metal sculpture which sprang directly from the gallery floor. Ignoring traditional sculptural materials, Caro used steel and aluminium in the form of plates, sheets, pipes, mesh and girders. Welding, riveting and bolting replaced the slower, traditional techniques of carving and modelling. Employing his material 'as found', Caro constructed his pieces from a miscellany of metal elements. The enclosed, solid, vertical forms of the past were rejected in favour of skeletal, open, linear, horizontal structures which activated the space surrounding them. Fried found these sculptures 'abstract and gestural', and was impressed by Caro's mastery of compositional syntax; Caro's work is always relational and this characteristic sets it apart from the Minimal structures of Judd, Morris and LeWitt.

At that time Caro covered his works with a uniform, monochromatic coat of paint. This custom was in marked contrast to the 'truth to materials' aesthetic of the past, and it puzzled the critics. They concluded that its purpose was to unify, to give an impression of weightlessness, and also to stress the opticality of the new sculpture rather than its tangibility. In the 1970s Caro has created a series of large, steel sculptures composed of angular planes which are heavier and tougher than his earlier pieces. Now Caro leaves the surfaces of his works unpainted and permits the dark greys of the steel and the reds of the accumulating rust to speak for themselves.

33

The example of Caro's work, and his presence in London as a tutor at St Martin's School of Art, inspired a number of young British sculptors. The first large public exhibition of their sculpture was the 1965 'New Generation' show which included work by David Annersley, Michael Bolus, Phillip King, Tim Scott, William Tucker, Isaac Witkin and Derrick Woodham; of the nine participants five had studied at St Martin's.

In contrast to the figurative 'geometry of fear' style, with its tortured surfaces and sombre colouration, that typified British sculpture in the 1950s, the new work was abstract, anonymously finished and brightly coloured; seen *en masse* it looked festive and playful. The young sculptors handled with confidence a range of materials – perspex, polyurethane, glass, steel, aluminium, fibreglass, wood – mostly chosen for their flexibility and because they permitted rapid execution.

One of the first British sculptors to capitalize on the advantages of plastics was Phillip King. A form which
28 intrigued King between 1963 and 1965 was the cone; he made it the subject of a series of major works. An American Minimal sculptor might have presented a cone as a pure form, but King subverted its structural integrity by hollowing it out, by slicing it vertically and by attaching to it oddly shaped appendages. Although these early works have no obvious repre-sentational content their enigmatic forms provoke an associational response. King's recent series of steel
27 sculptures, *Red Between*, *Blue Between* and *Yellow Between* (1971–73), have the same characteristic; in this instance their diversity of form and complication of structure irresistibly suggests analogies with plant morphology.

American critics sarcastically describe the 'New Generation' sculptors as 'British lightweights', and, reluctantly, one must admit that nine years later their work seems dated, its glossy brightness shallow and its optimism misplaced. However, what Caro, King and Tucker did achieve in 1960–65 was to lay the foundations of a sophisticated sculptural language – not the old 'grammar of forms' but a complex of syntactical relationships – which activates the viewer's kinaesthetic sense: the inbuilt knowledge of movement derived from muscles, tendons and joints. Great sculpture has always evoked a bodily response, but the sculptural language has never before evinced itself in so pure a form, nor has it communicated itself so exclusively through vision rather than touch.

34 Consider the formal clarity of Tucker's *Beulah* series (1971–72). Physically the sculptures consist of lengths of steel tubing that have been twisted into sinuous shapes. They depart radically from what Tucker terms 'the enclosed object aesthetic' by being completely open in form: they resemble drawings in space and 'breathe' because the space which they articulate is nowhere confined. The lightness, economy and fluency of Tucker's recent work has few precedents.

William Turnbull is two years older than Caro. For twenty-five years he has worked steadily within the international mainstream of Modernism, but, because the British revere eccentricity in art above all else, for most of his career Turnbull remained an underrated artist. He displays equal facility as a painter and as a sculptor, but has always retained a clear distinction between the two media. During the mid-1950s his sculpture passed through a totemic phase that reflected the influence of primitive art; these works were figurative and possessed highly textured surfaces. Later in the decade he produced a series of abstract monochromatic paintings in which the materiality of the paint and its method of application, by brush and palette knife, was stressed. By the early 1960s his totems had become simpler but bulkier: they were made up from rounded blocks of stone, wood and bronze stacked on top of one another in various permutations. Much of the appeal of these works depended upon the contrast of one material against another.

In the last decade Turnbull has abandoned all figurative references and committed himself wholeheartedly to the American Minimal aesthetic. As Richard Morphet pointed out, on the occasion of Turnbull's retrospective at the Tate Gallery in 1973, the artist is obsessed by 'the integrity of the unit'. His current works are static, symmetrical, and have an industrial finish; they exemplify wholeness.

29

In becoming a competent exponent of Minimalism, Turnbull has sacrificed the individuality and originality of his earlier work: in the drive to total abstraction, meaning has progressively drained away from his sculpture; and Morphet's claim that Turnbull's is a 'matter of fact' art, which appeals to the 'ordinarily imaginative person', seems to me spurious.

Less = more: Minimal art

In Stanley Kubrick's *2001: A Space Odyssey* (1968) a mysterious, polished, black rectangular monolith constructed by alien beings from the stars appears on Earth and imparts intelligence to the forebears of the human race. Through this film a mass audience was introduced to an artifact which exhibited all the characteristics of a Minimal art object.

The term 'Minimal art' was coined by the philosopher Richard Wollheim in 1965 to describe a particular kind of twentieth-century art object: those with a very low art-content, for example, the paintings of Ad Reinhardt and the readymades of Marcel Duchamp. Later the term came to refer, more specifically, to three-dimensional objects produced by certain American artists in the early and mid-1960s.

An alternative description (in the latter sense), 'Structural' or 'Structurist art', derives from the title of an exhibition held at the Jewish Museum, New York, in 1966: 'Primary Structures'. This important show featured sculpture by the American artists Carl Andre, Richard Artschwager, Larry Bell, Ronald Bladen, Walter de Maria, Dan Flavin, Robert Grosvenor, Douglas Huebler, Donald Judd, Ellsworth Kelly, Sol LeWitt, John McCracken, Robert Morris, Robert Smithson and others. British sculpture was represented by Caro and several of the 'New Generation' school, but it is now clear that their work was not structural in intent.

In 1968 the art critic Barbara Reise claimed that Wollheim's term 'Minimal' was 'linguistically reprehensible' because it referred to a 'quantity of art rather than to a set of stylistic characteristics'. Nevertheless certain common qualities can be identified in the work of the American sculptors who showed at the Jewish Museum, namely total abstraction, order, simplicity, clarity, factory fabrication, a high degree of finish and anti-illusionism or literalness. Like Stella, the Minimal sculptors rejected the European tradition of internal, part to part, hierarchical relationships – the Cubist aesthetic – on the grounds that it was fundamentally anthropomorphic. They presented instead elementary geometric forms whose shapes could be understood at a glance, whose image was co-extensive with their structure. The cube, or box, became the most hackneyed of these forms: Tony Smith's *Die*, 1962 (a six-foot steel cube), Robert Morris's *Untitled 1965* (boxes with mirror surfaces),
21 Larry Bell's series of semi-transparent glass cubes. Because such objects had virtually no incident, and apparently no complexity, viewers found them inert, sterile and boring. (However, boredom is presumably just as legitimate an emotion for art to evoke as any other; nor was its use restricted to the Minimalists: Pop artists such as Andy Warhol also exploited the novelty value of tedium.)

When we study an art object with as little visual appeal as a steel cube our aesthetic interest tends to shift from internal to external relationships, for example to the relationship between our ideal mental concept 'cube' and the constantly altering shape and illumination of the actual cube as we look at it and move around it. Therefore Minimal art, like Op art, though more subtly, invoked the viewer's perceptual experience (this fact prompted certain critics to interpret it in terms of Maurice Merleau-Ponty's phenomenology). Interest also shifts to the relationship between the art object and the negative space of its architectural setting: as Carl Andre points out, a sculpture is above all else a 'cut in space'. Increasingly, Minimal artists created sculpture to suit a particular gallery; consequently the total installation became the primary focus of attention rather than the separate items of which it was composed. As a result art exhibits became non-transferable and depended on the artist's ability to repeat a 'performance'.

It is ironic that the ideology of Ad Reinhardt – the veteran abstract painter of the New York School who died in 1967 – should have corresponded so closely to that of the Minimalists; he had a total contempt for sculpture, and once defined it as 'something you bump into when you back up to look at a painting'.

During the last six years of his life Reinhardt produced a series of paintings that were identical in format: they were all five feet square and contained a simple cruciform image. Their colouration was extremely dark, and the variations of colour and tone between the parts of the image so slight that at first sight the paintings appear to be uniform expanses of black paint. However, if time is allowed for the eye to adjust to the subtle differences of value, then the image becomes visible. Reproductions give no indication of the merit of these works; indeed it was Reinhardt's deliberate intention to thwart the easy assimilation of his art via illustrations in art magazines.

Critics have described Reinhardt's late paintings as 'invisible', but he preferred to use the adjective 'ultimate', because he believed that they were 'the last paintings that anyone could make'. Reinhardt subscribed to Greenberg's 'pure painting' thesis: he was vehemently opposed to the adulteration of painting by any other art, and he progressively reduced his pictorial means until he had arrived at an ultimate point beyond which no further abstraction, within the art of painting, was feasible. John Stezaker describes Reinhardt's reductionism, or rejective approach, and that of Minimal art generally, as a 'programme of forbearance': 'It's not what you put in that counts, it's what you leave out.'

Perhaps of more importance than Reinhardt's paintings, to the younger generation of Minimal and Conceptual artists of the 1960s, were the polemical writings in which he expounded his 'art-as-art' dogma. Reinhardt maintained that art had no meaning outside itself, and also that its meaning could not be translated into any other medium; consequently, the only way he could comment on art, except via his painting, was by means of absolute, *negative* statements and elaborate cartoons on the art world.

Donald Judd has been described as 'the extreme structurist' because of the radical simplicity of his three-dimensional objects. His best known sculpture, 24 *Untitled* (Minimal artists constantly affirm the non-referential character of their objects – no illusions, no allusions – by employing the opaque and cryptic title *'Untitled'*), consists of a series of chunky iron boxes set at nine-inch intervals on a wall to form a vertical row. In his writings Judd emphasizes their non-relational order, but he also stresses that this order is not 'rationalistic'; it is, he says, 'simply order'. *Untitled* can be regarded as a segment taken from a continuum, and the arbitrariness of the length of this segment is confirmed by Judd's instruction to gallery staff that the number of boxes hung may be varied to suit different ceiling heights.

If we compare Judd's objects with a sculpture such as Barnett Newman's *Broken Obelisk*, the extent of the

Barnett Newman (1905–70). *Broken Obelisk*, 1963–67.
Corten steel, 26ft × 10ft 6 × 10ft 6 (7.93 × 3.20 × 3.20m).
Seagram Building, New York.

Minimalists' departure from the mainstream of modern sculpture becomes clear. Newman's huge work, executed in 1967, consists of a pyramid on whose apex a 'broken' obelisk is impaled. Although Newman's two forms are individually as simple as those favoured by Minimal artists, their references to Egyptian art, their symbolic overtones and the dynamic energy of their interaction is in marked contrast to the chic hermeticism of most primary structures.

One of the reasons Judd gave for preferring the third to the second dimension was the opportunity of using all sorts of materials and colours, and, in particular, the new products made available by modern technology, such as plexiglass, stainless steel, formica, aluminium and galvanized iron. Judd was attracted by their non-art quality, their aggressiveness and specificity; he wanted to emphasize their physical character and to retain their 'obdurate identity'. He pushed the 'truth to materials' adage to a new extreme of literalness in the belief that the identity of the art object could be made to coincide with its constituents.

Sol LeWitt is not so obsessed by materials. His elegant rectilinear structures exploit the contrast between conceptual order and visual disorder. For example, the sculpture *Series A*, 1967 (the first of a set of four structures in which a progression from open to enclosed form is completely exhausted), is logically simple; but, because of the effects of perspective, cast shadows and the way parts of the framework overlap when it is seen, it is perceptually extremely complex. *Series A* employs the same kind of 'order' as Judd's objects: it is based on a grid which, as LeWitt explains in a note in the margin of one of his plans, 'is a convenience. It stabilizes the measurements and neutralizes space by treating it equally'. Subsequently the grid device became a cliché of the art of the late 1960s, especially in painting (so much so that in 1972 a whole exhibition was mounted in the United States devoted to work using grids).

Sol LeWitt (1928–). *Series A,* 1967. 24ft × 24ft × 6ft 9 (7.32 × 7.32 × 2.06m). Photo John Weber Gallery, New York.

LeWitt's sculptures were fabricated by industrial companies working from his specifications. This method of production was commonplace among Minimal artists and explains the lack of handwork in their sculptures (this is why the term 'art object' is often preferred to 'work of art' or 'artwork' in this context). The role of specifications in sculpture was equivalent to that of scores in music.

Because of the importance of the conceptual element in LeWitt's sculptures they have been described as 'Idea art'; and he himself once explained that an idea was a 'machine that makes the work'. He also wrote in 1968 the seminal document 'Sentences on Conceptual Art'; but LeWitt is not strictly speaking a Conceptual artist, because he continues to relish the ambiguity between concept and object – unlike his successors, who regard specifications and the objects which they generate as merely two different physical forms of presentation of mental concepts.

39 LeWitt is particularly noted for his wall drawings and prints; like his sculpture, these are generated by sets of rules designed to exclude taste, accident and the artist's personal 'handwriting'. The drawings are often executed by students or other artists working from LeWitt's written instructions. Minimal art does not usually exhibit the quality of beauty, but LeWitt's drawings are an exception. Their richness proves that less can, on occasion, equal more. They also illustrate the knack American artists possess of solving formal problems at a stroke. For example, a perennial issue confronting all draughtsmen is how to relate colour and line. LeWitt's solution is absurdly simple: coloured lines.

19, 20 Another artist who relies on the products of industry is Dan Flavin, but he does not need to send out specifications to be made up by others, because he purchases readymade fluorescent light fixtures. By choosing an illuminated tube as the basic unit of his art, Flavin telescopes material, light, colour and space into a single entity.

Light artists are generally linked with Kinetic art; but Flavin has no interest in movement or changes in luminosity. His light sculpture is always presented in a fixed, static form; if his art relates to any tradition it is that of Constructivism. Flavin's early lamps were arranged vertically on walls in a manner reminiscent of the format of Barnett Newman's paintings. He quickly realized that their effect was to break down the space of the rooms in which they were placed, and he has since modulated room spaces by siting his radiant bars of colour across corners and also by building them into free-standing 'barrier structures'.

21 The sculptures of Larry Bell, a Los Angeles artist, also modulate light, but indirectly, through the

medium of glass which has been made semi-transparent by being vacuum-coated with metallic compounds, a process Bell controls by using heavy machinery installed in his factory-like studio. His famous series of mirrored and translucent glass cubes date from 1964; since then he has created numerous 'bevel strip' pieces that reflect tints of colour on to the walls on which they are mounted. He has also linked large, subtly toned glass panels together to form maze-like structures which multiply reflections and fuse mysteriously with their environments. These cool, elusive, exquisite works display the refinement of finish characteristic of Los Angeles art.

In recent years Bell, and other West Coast artists such as Michael Asher, Robert Irwin, Bruce Nauman and Doug Wheeler, have designed indoor environments which totally surround the viewer. These environments can be categorized as Minimal art because their visual incident is so slight that the viewer's own phenomenological experience of light, space and duration constitute the artwork.

In appearance, Minimal art objects closely resemble the 'good design' of modular furniture and household appliances and the austere forms of 'functional' architecture. By exemplifying 'standardization, repetition and repeatability' (Robert Morris's words), they faithfully reflect the ethos of Western industrial society. Similarly, the popularity of systematic procedures and serial ordering in American art of the 1960s – demonstrated by the exhibitions 'Systemic Painting' (1966), 'Art in Series' (1967) and 'Serial Imagery' (1968) – echoed the logic and methodology of the applied sciences and business management.

In his essay 'Time in the Museum', Harold Rosenberg described the immaculate neatness of Post-Painterly Abstraction and Minimal art as an 'aesthetic of cleanliness' exemplifying middle-class values of tidiness and security. During the second half of the 1960s the hegemony of Minimal and formalist aesthetics began to decline as more and more artists developed increasingly eccentric modes of art in their attempts to escape from the spiral of reductionism that so quickly produced blank canvases and mute objects.

Beyond the object (1): Process art

Sculptors have traditionally favoured hard, durable materials in order to create rigid objects that remain constant in form. However, no sooner had Minimal art established itself publicly than a different attitude to form and a more catholic approach to materials was manifested in a number of exhibitions held in the United States – 'Eccentric Abstraction' (1966), 'Earthworks', 'Anti-Form', '9 at Leo Castelli' (1968), 'Anti-illusion' (1969) – and in Europe – 'Art Povera' (1967/68), 'Op Losse Schroven', 'When Attitudes Become Form' (1969). Among the artists participating in these shows were Carl Andre, Giovanni Anselmo, Joseph Beuys, Alighiero Boetti, Louise Bourgeois, Rafael Ferrer, Barry Flanagan, Eva Hesse, Hans Haacke, Jannis Kounellis, Mario Merz, Robert Morris, Bruce Nauman, Reiner Ruthenbeck, Richard Serra and Keith Sonnier.

The work of Eva Hesse, a gifted artist who died in 1970 at the age of thirty-four, contributed greatly to the establishment of a viable Post-Minimal aesthetic. Usually her sculpture consisted of mixtures of cheap materials, and her techniques included several in which women are conventionally supposed to excel: sewing, lacing, bandaging. Her forms were idiosyncratic and frequently humorous; they were coarsely textured, irregular and tenuous. Since she preferred limp substances her works often dangled like webs from walls or ceilings. Hesse's sculptures reflected the influence of Surrealism and of Oldenburg's soft sculptures; unlike the non-referential structures of her friend Sol LeWitt, they had organic, visceral and sexual connotations.

44

The exhibitions mentioned above contained an immense variety of work; but all featured abstract sculptures composed of unexpected materials, including grass, ice, soil, felt, cement, stones, rubber, graphite, grease and coal, which were often incongruously collocated. Used directly, such materials tend to accumulate into heaps or clumps; they lend themselves to stacking, scattering, smearing and draping. Therefore the sculptures revealed the processes involved in their construction, and also reflected the influence of natural forces, especially gravity; often the sculptures exemplified impermanence by deteriorating with the passage of time.

The forms of the new sculpture seemed, in comparison to the predominantly rectilinear, ordered and geometric objects of the immediate past, randomly composed and amorphous. Yet however different the new sculpture may have appeared, it was in fact the mirror image of Minimal art: its impermanence and variable form were simply the timelessness and structural stability of Minimal sculpture in reverse.

Pre-eminent among the American artists who effected this reversal of terms was the inventive and prolific sculptor, dancer and writer Robert Morris. The range and diversity of his output is astonishing. In the early 1960s he created mixed-media sculptures inspired by Duchamp and Johns, and simultaneously made Minimal primary structures; in 1967 he produced rigid permutational units and also floppy pieces made from felt; in 1968 and 1969 he created 'anti-form' sculptures, including one utilizing steam; in 1971 he constructed in Holland a huge earthwork entitled *Observatory* and devised participatory sculptures for his show at the Tate Gallery, London; in 1972 he created *Hearing*, a complex symbolic tableau accompanied by a tape-recorded dialogue.

An early work – a wooden box containing a recording of the sound of its construction – discloses the recurrent theme of his art: the compulsion to

41

22

Ian Burn (1939–   ). *Xerox Book,* 1968. Courtesy of the artist.

dramatize the act of making. So it is not surprising that in the late 1960s Morris was a leading exponent of Process art: art in which making procedures are treated as subject matter, in which 'means' become 'ends'. Usually fairly simple techniques are employed, so that the viewer can mentally reconstruct from the final work the methods employed. Typical examples include: a shotgun fired at a wall, the result photographed and enlarged, a second shot fired at the enlarged photograph, the result photographed . . . (Morris); molten lead repeatedly poured along the junction of wall and floor, the resulting angular forms displayed as sculpture (Richard Serra); two minutes of spray paint directly on a floor from a standard aerosol can (Lawrence Weiner); a blank sheet of white paper copied in a Xerox machine, the copy used to make a second copy, this process repeated one hundred times, the result – papers with ever increasing texture – bound and presented in book form (Ian Burn).

The origins of the Process idiom can be traced to the Surrealists and their 'automatism', or abandonment of conscious control; more direct influences in America were the drip-painting method of Jackson Pollock and the pouring technique of Morris Louis.

34

What interested Morris and others about automatism was not its power to reveal the unconscious mind but the possibility of an *automated* method of creation that would permit, in Morris's words, 'art making . . . based on other terms than those arbitrary, formalistic, tasteful arrangements of static forms'. Once the Process artist has decided on a systematic method his behaviour becomes automatic, and the results are accepted, without regard to their visual appeal, as if they were natural products.

Back to nature: Earth, Land and ecological art

The vogue for Earth art began with the habit of dumping quantities of granular matter on to the floors of art galleries. This tendency was carried to its logical conclusion by Walter de Maria who deposited, in 1968, 1,600 cubic feet of soil inside a gallery blanketing the whole floor area. Artists such as Robert Smithson, Michael Heizer, Carl Andre and Richard Long became interested in the sculptural potential of the excavations from which they derived their gravel, rocks and earth.

Earth artists were released from the space restrictions of studios and galleries and escaped, momentarily, the precious-object marketing system of art. Therefore they were able to create with the aid of bulldozers, dynamite and digging machinery grandiose earthworks and immense excavations: Morris's *Observatory* was 230 feet across and took several months to build; Smithson's *Spiral Jetty*, composed of rocks dumped in the waters of the Great Salt Lake, Utah, was 1,500 feet in length; Heizer's *Double Negative* (1969–70), located in Nevada, involved the removal of 240,000 tons of rock and sand.

41
40

42

Morris's structure was designed to function, like Stonehenge, as a solar calendar, and it seems more than coincidental that earthworks were produced during a period when a passion for prehistoric mounds, monuments and leys developed among members of the Underground subculture. Although Richard Long is exceedingly reticent about his work, his documentation reveals a connection by including photographs of the Bronze Age earthwork at Silbury Hill, and of ancient hill figures.

Land art marked a shift away from the sculptural emphasis on 'actual' materials, derived from Minimal aesthetics, towards a more pictorial approach in which artists inscribed designs on the land surface. De Maria chalked lines a mile in length in the desert; Long 'drew' lines in grass by walking back and forth and by cutting off the heads of daisies; Dennis Oppenheim cut curved channels in the ice of a frozen lake and created large-scale patterns by supervising the planting and harvesting of farm crops. Frequently such works could be appreciated in their entirety only from the air, because of their gigantic size or because of their isolated locations. The necessity for Land artists to use aircraft had tragic consequences for Robert Smithson: he was killed in a plane crash in 1973 while surveying the site for a new sculpture.

Most examples of Land art are not transportable – though Long usually works on a modest scale and some of his pieces have been installed in galleries – nor are they physically accessible to a majority of the urban art public. Documentation in the form of maps, photographs, booklets and videotapes, therefore assumes a crucial role. Ironically, the originality of the works themselves was often negated by the conventional way documentation was displayed in art galleries. As the carefully contrived nostalgia, and English romanticism, of Long's and Hamish Fulton's landscape photographs demonstrate, Land artists became deeply interested in the secondary, presentational aspects of their art.

The Land artists' sentimental attachment to the picturesque has provoked certain critics to a frenzy of sarcasm. More specifically, Land artists have been

Richard Long (1945–). *England*, 1968. Sculpture made by removing daisy heads from a field. Courtesy of the artist and Lisson Gallery.

criticized for being, from the formal point of view, retrogressive: in spite of their apparently radical step of using nature as an art material, the simple patterns they impose on nature are generally banal designs originating from geometric abstract painting.

In certain respects the work of Long and Fulton overlaps with that of Process and Performance artists in that they indulge in forms of ritualized behaviour, often demanding great endurance, for example, walking, running, cycling or swimming for pre-determined times or distances.

Jan Dibbets, Holland's leading artist, abandoned painting in 1967, having reached, by the now familiar reductive method, the blank canvas impasse. His subsequent work, exploiting such media as photography, tape-recording, film, postal systems, maps and videotape, has on occasion been classed as 'Land art' because its overt subject matter was the natural elements of air, earth, fire and water. However,

Dibbets' range is much broader than most Land art: the themes of his art include perspective, illusion, light, movement and time.

Like Long and Fulton, Dibbets often presents sequences of photographs; but his are not merely tasteful records: they are integral to his work. For example, in his 'perspective correction' series, the trapezoid shapes which Dibbets cuts in grass or draws on walls can be seen as a square only from one vantage point, which the camera 'freezes'. The resulting photographic image displays a spatial ambiguity not available in reality: the image can be read as a square on the surface plane of the photo, or, alternatively, it can be read in depth as a trapezoid.

Not the least of Dibbets' accomplishments is his wit. In 1969 he commented on the domestic habits of the bourgeoisie by transforming thousands of household TV sets into 'fireplaces': he showed a twenty-four-minute film of a fire on a public television network; as in Warhol's early films, viewing time equalled filming time. By manipulating the angle and direction of his camera while taking a sequence of photographs of the flat horizons of Holland, Dibbets has also created 'Dutch mountains'.

Despite the variety of concepts and media that Dibbets employs his art remains essentially visual and pictorial; his dispassionate view of nature continues the landscape tradition of seventeenth-century Dutch painting.

Oppenheim's agricultural projects utilized the cyclical systems of nature. In fact, during the late 1960s and early 1970s when public consciousness of environmental or ecological issues was at its height, a number of artists including Hans Haacke, Newton Harrison, Peter Hutchinson, Luis F. Benedit, Robert Irwin, Gordon Matta, David Medalla, Charles Ross, Alan Sonfist, Takis and John Van Saun, isolated physical and biological systems and presented them as artworks. For example, in 1971 Harrison exhibited

Jan Dibbets (1941–　). *Perspective Correction,* 1969. Section cut out from grass.

a portable fish farm at the Hayward Gallery, London; a furore was caused by his proposal to electrocute catfish in public.

Haacke, a German resident in the United States whose interest in systems dates from the early 1960s, has created equally controversial works. He began by exploring inorganic and organic systems, but more recently he has turned his attention to social phenomena; for example, in 1970 he conducted a poll of museum visitors concerning a socio-political issue of the day, and in the following year he documented the ownership of slum property in New York; although Haacke's presentation was completely objective the information proved too radical for the Guggenheim Museum, which refused to display it.

43

An alternative to fine art: freak culture

Although the sensibility of the international youth culture which emerged during the second half of the 1960s expressed itself primarily through pop music and clothing, it also manifested itself, to a significant extent, in the visual arts. Generally the artists who served the Underground sub-culture were members of it and therefore shared the same tastes as their prospective audience. Their creations ranged from psychedelic and visionary paintings, light shows, posters, magazine illustrations and layouts, comic books, record sleeve designs, to various kinds of handicraft. What distinguished Underground art from the products of fine artists previously discussed was an emphasis on graphic imagery, a priority of content over form, and the desire to reach a much wider, less exclusive, audience by using printed media capable of providing cheap, unlimited editions.

The aim of the Underground was to alter states of consciousness; the short cuts to this goal were acid, marijuana and pills. The Psychedelic painter sought to communicate, via a visual analogue, his hallucinogenic drug experience, or to provide an object of contemplation for those under the influence of drugs. Without the gloss of the drug experience most Psychedelic paintings are aesthetically puerile. Their stylistic characteristics – all-over decorative patterning, a *mélange* of abstract and figurative motifs, snaky dissolving forms, ambiguous spatial effects, iridescent and acidic colours – aiming at what Timothy Leary called 'retinal orgasm' – were also typical of Underground poster art and graphic design.

A more appropriate medium than painting or graphics for the kaleidoscopic effects sought by the Psychedelic painters was the light show, which became mandatory at all pop music venues. Sound, coloured smoke, slide projections and stroboscopic lights were used by multi-media groups such as

53 USCO and Mark Boyle's Sensual Laboratory to induce synaesthesia by bombarding several senses simultaneously. By amplifying the sound of the music to ear-deafening levels, and by tuning the oscillations of the strobe light to the frequency of brain rhythms, they succeeded in disorientating normal consciousness and provided, in effect, a synthetic trip.

Alan Aldridge, Michael English and Martin Sharp are three illustrators whose reputations have survived the demise of the Underground and its press. Sharp, an Australian who worked chiefly for *Oz* magazine, produced two classic examples of the cult-hero

54 poster eulogizing Bob Dylan and Vincent Van Gogh. Underground artists invariably exhibited a magpie eclecticism, and Sharp's recent collages, which he calls 'artoons' – ironic juxtapositions of images clipped from reproductions of famous paintings – continue this tendency.

Perhaps the most potent vehicle for the dissemination of the ethos of the Underground was the so-called 'head' comic book. *Zap*, the first important title, appeared in California, the homeland of Psychedelic art, Flower Power, Hippies and Freak Culture, in 1968. It was drawn by the one indisputable genius of the Underground, Robert Crumb. The comic strip form enabled Crumb to present the social and political issues of the day in a vivid and entertaining manner. As an observer of the mores of American society, and, above all, the frowzy Hippy life-style, he has no equal.

Crumb shares with Dickens an ability to invent memorable characters: Fritz the Cat, Mr Natural, Whiteman, Angelfood McSpade, Honeybunch Kaminski and Lenore Goldberg. Unblinkingly he depicts their obscene behaviour and violent atrocities, and his cartoons act as a cathartic for the sadistic fantasies of his readers. Morally Crumb remains neutral – he gives no sign of approval or disapproval of what happens in his strips – and this endows them with a disturbing ambiguity.

The highly distinctive drawing style which Crumb has evolved – thick, heavy delineations of bulbous forms – exactly complements his subject matter. (Another artist who has deliberately adopted a crude, 'amateurish style of drawing is the Austrian Günter Brus; his works depict even more violent and pornographic scenes than Crumb's.) The funky, 'all-meat' comic books of Robert Crumb provide a welcome contrast to the cerebral research pamphlets published by many of the Conceptual artists discussed later.

Recent painting: comeback or collapse?

Pundits have informed us that painting is dead; but, perversely, its corpse will not rest. However, if reviving past styles is a sign of decadence, then the paintings which the American artists David Diao, Robert Duran, Alan Shields, Ken Showell, James Sullivan, David Cummings, Donald Lewallen and others produced at the end of the 1960s must be counted as decadent: they re-appraise the Abstract Expressionism of the 1950s and its European equivalent, *art informel*.

55   The New Informalists, as Carter Ratcliff labelled them, adopted the large formats, the all-over configurations, and the process-orientated work methods of their predecessors, but scrupulously avoided their emotional commitment. The intention now was decorative. Acrylic pigments were applied in multiple layers by staining and spraying, or by using squeegees; the results were extremely colourful, variously textured, illusionistic, and in general somewhat pretty (one critic dismissed them as 'visual Muzak'). As Ratcliff pointed out, their soft-focus lyricism reflected the dreamy, drug-conditioned consciousness that was also manifested in the late-1960s vogue for batik and tie-dyed fabrics.

There are some conscientious British artists – for example John Walker and John Hoyland – who remain convinced that there is mileage left in painting, in particular Abstract Expressionist or Action painting, and they express their opinion over miles of canvas. Walker, a prizewinner at the John Moores Liverpool exhibition in 1965, has flirted with grids and shaped canvases. He confesses that he is in love with the act of painting, and often employs a variety of methods of paint application within one picture. His recent work explores the florid 'handwriting' aspect of Action painting. Hoyland delights in the viscosity of acrylic pigments, and the by-product of his liberal application of paint to rectangular forms in the centre of his canvases is a fringe of nostalgic drips and dribbles.

Periodically a fresh generation of painters finds it necessary to confront that great nineteenth-century rival of painting, photography. The latest attempt at assimilation, known as Photo-Realism, developed quietly throughout the 1960s and only emerged as a fully fledged style in 1972 when it was shown in force at the vast 'Documenta 5' at Kassel, an exhibition devoted to the theme of 'questioning reality'.

Well known Photo-Realists include Robert Bechtle, Claudio Bravo, John Clem Clarke, Chuck Close, Robert Cottingham, Don Eddy, Richard Estes, Bruce Everett, Franz Gertsch, Ralph Goings, Michael Gorman, John Kacere, Alfred Leslie, Richard McLean, Malcolm Morley and John Salt. This list of names reveals the international character of the style, though the majority of the artists are, as one might expect, American. The multifarious German painter Gerhard Richter has also produced many canvases based on blurred photographs. A major British painter whose recent work is heavily dependent upon photographs is David Hockney. The graffiti-inspired imagery of his early paintings was flatly drawn and highly stylized, and his brushstrokes were spontaneous

56

52, 51
48

49

slashes; but since 1964 he has moved in the direction of straightforward naturalism, and has tightened up his brushwork to procure a greater degree of finish. Hockney frankly admits that his painting has become more conventional.

47   Most Photo-Realists use photographs as an impersonal source of visual imagery. Because their attitude to subject content is neutral, they prefer reportage photographs of banal motifs: urban landscapes, automobiles, shop fronts, horses and faces. Clarke and Morley also revamp coloured reproductions of old masterpieces. The photographs are meticulously copied in acrylic paint; the prefixes 'Super-', 'Radical', 'Hyper-' and 'Sharp-focus' have been applied to this realism because of its extreme verisimilitude and thoroughness of technique. Often the scale of

48   Photo-Realist canvases is monumental, matching that of Abstract Expressionism; their inflated size and cold, mechanical finish endows them with a disturbing quality which recalls Surrealist painting.

Photo-Realists are not interested in photographic realism (in the sense that realist painters such as Andrew Wyeth and Alex Colville seek to emulate the detailed accuracy of camera vision). To them photographs are simply flat images for use on flat planes. What intrigues the Photo-Realists is the technical problems of rendering tones across a surface and

51   capturing highlights and reflections. They treat all parts of the image impartially: Morley turns his photographs sideways to negate their subject matter, and also cuts them into small squares for transposing to canvas. Therefore Photo-Realism is in some respects more akin to formalist abstraction than to the tradition of realist painting.

50   Verist sculpture, the three-dimensional equivalent of Photo-Realism, depends upon the technique of making casts from the human body in fibreglass and polyester resin. American practitioners, such as John De Andrea and Duane Hanson, frequently devise

Robert Ryman (1930–   ). *Untitled*, 1965. Oil on cotton, 10 × 10 (25.4 × 25.4). Collection the artist.

narrative tableaux, with horrific or political themes, composed of groups of life-size figures dressed in genuine clothes. In spite of the use of real clothes and other props, the literal character of sculpture militates against complete illusionism, and when they are seen 'in the flesh' these petrified tableaux often fail to carry conviction: they occupy a twilight zone between artifice and reality. Ironically, they are more effective in photographs.

'Minimal' or 'Cool' painting and drawing, whose progress in the 1960s was overshadowed by Minimal sculpture and the emergence of Conceptual art, is at last receiving the critical attention it merits. Besides the Olitski and Kelly retrospectives of 1973, there have been exhibitions devoted to Robert Ryman (1972) and Agnes Martin (1973) in the United States, and recent mixed exhibitions in Europe have shown the work of Kelly, Brice Marden, Jo Baer, Ralph Humphrey and Robert Mangold.

Minimal paintings are daunting in their austerity: typically, they are monochrome canvases consisting of white paint on a white ground. Their meaning is wholly concentrated in the artist's choice of materials, in the interaction of the physical characteristics of these materials, and in the slight manipulation of materials which Minimal painters permit themselves. Ryman, for example, employs a wide range of materials in order to exploit such contrasts as opaque/translucent, shiny/matt, smooth/rough and thick/thin. When applying pigment he restricts himself to the quintessential brushstroke and repeats it until he has filled his square canvases with a series of horizontal, parallel strokes of paint.

Douglas Crimp has introduced the term 'Opaque painting'. He argues that all the devices adopted by Minimal painters – the neutral formats and colours, the non-relational grids, the direct use of materials, the removal of stretchers to stress that painting is simply pigment on cloth, and above all the quality of opacity – are intended to negate illusionism and to match the literalness of 'specific objects' by developing 'specific surfaces'.

Other artists resort to different strategies in order to cope with the 'bankruptcy' of painting. Tom Phillips, a skilful English painter, plunders art history for styles and techniques, blends abstraction and figuration, and also makes use of lettering, photographs and postcard views. Although his pictures are charming and cleverly orchestrated (he is also a musician), they are rather precious; Phillips' catholicity and pluralism masks his lack of an ideology.

In France ideological commitment in art is taken literally. Marc Devade and Louis Cane are two French painters who have developed a style based on a re-evaluation of Newman, Rothko and Louis. Vis-

36

Daniel Buren (1938–   ). *Photo/Souvenir, Paris, April, 1968.*

ually the paintings are conventional enough; what is unusual about them is their critical back-up. Devade and Cane are members of a polemical group called Supports/Surfaces, and publish a journal devoted to the theory of painting. Strangely, their formalistic pictorial practice is supported by theory incorporating the dialectical materialism of Marx and the thoughts of Chairman Mao.

Mark Lancaster, an Englishman, and Ron Davis, an American, are representative of a type of abstract painter whose work tastefully amalgamates several fashionable ideas of the 1960s. Lancaster's paintings exhibit an intelligent appreciation of grid structures, process techniques, and the Art Deco style; Davis's fibreglass wallpieces incorporate the shaped canvas concept, abstract illusionism and, more recently, the decorative splashing of the Informalist revival. Such hybrid solutions are not for Daniel Buren. This French artist is Reinhardt's natural heir. Rejecting composition, style and formal development, Buren proclaims his total rupture with the painting of the

37

35

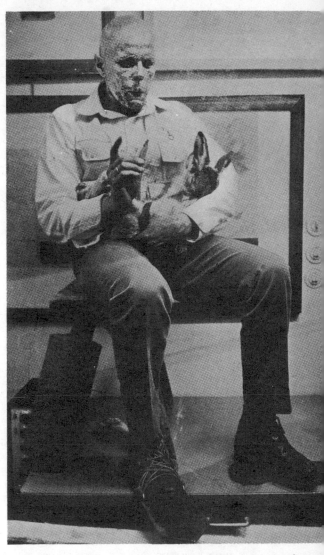

Joseph Beuys (1921–   ). *How to Explain Pictures to a Dead Hare*, 1965. Action at Galerie Schmela, Düsseldorf.

past by manufacturing the 'same' painting over and over again: since 1966 he has created works always containing vertical stripes 8.7 cm wide, alternately white and coloured. Although this format is never varied internally, Buren provides variety externally by changing the physical location of his pieces. It is ironic that the stripes which Buren selected because they were 'neutral' and 'anonymous' are now instantly recognizable, in whatever context, as his personal trademark.

38   Another artist whose work has a conceptual bias is the Japanese born painter Shusaku Arakawa. Instead of depicting objects Arakawa stencils their names on to canvas. Often his paintings contain questions, equations, contradictory statements, or absurd instructions; once he invited the viewer to steal the painting (this duly happened). Arakawa's declared intention is to melt language systems into each other, in particular, written language and the 'language' of pictorial representation.

There seems no intrinsic reason why painting should not thrive; after all, its potential as a channel for information is infinite. But at the moment painting is neglected by the most original artists because they refuse to accept the imperatives of any one medium.

Beyond the object (2): actions and Body art

One of the few European artists whose charisma rivals that of leading New York artists, such as Andy Warhol, is the German Joseph Beuys. He trained as a sculptor and became an apostle of mixed-media pieces made from 'poor' materials; his favourite substance was fat. In the early 1960s Beuys and his compatriot Wolf Vostell were associated with the loose-knit international community of artists known as Fluxus, a non-conformist grouping noted for their Happenings, actions, publishing, and mailing activities.

60

Through his enigmatic actions, sculptures, drawings and multiples, Beuys established his reputation as an artist; but his public notoriety is a result of his fierce determination to merge art and life. One critic called him a 'cultural stormtrooper'. In 1967 he founded the German Student Party, and in 1971 the Organization of Non-Voters: both political organizations. In 1972 he was dismissed from his post at the Düsseldorf Academy because of the chaos caused by putting his educational theories into practice. Beuys is convinced that individual freedom can be achieved only through creativity. He believes that his duty as an artist is to educate, and so his recent actions consist of Beuys – wearing, as always, his famous hat and waistcoat – talking to an audience for twelve hours at a stretch and illustrating his concepts, as schoolmasters do, by drawing in chalk on a blackboard.

Very different from Beuys' Utopian actions are those of a group of Viennese artists 'exiled' in Germany – Günter Brus, Otto Mühl, Hermann Nitsch and Rudolf Schwarzkogler – some of whom took part in the Destruction in Art movement which reached a climax in London in 1966. Their actions are lengthy, brutal, obscene ceremonies, usually involving the smearing of blood and entrails of eviscerated animals over the naked bodies of participants. Although the intention of these appalling scenes is to highlight the violence of man and to act as a form of shock-therapy, their ethical basis is dubious. The Austrians feel that representing reality via a medium is no longer meaningful and the central idea behind their rituals is 'material action', that is, using reality itself as a means of formal creation. Thus their art consists of direct, literal events, not make-believe performances. The deadly seriousness of their aesthetic is indicated by the fact that Schwarzkogler (1940–69) killed himself in the name of art by successive acts of self-mutilation.

58

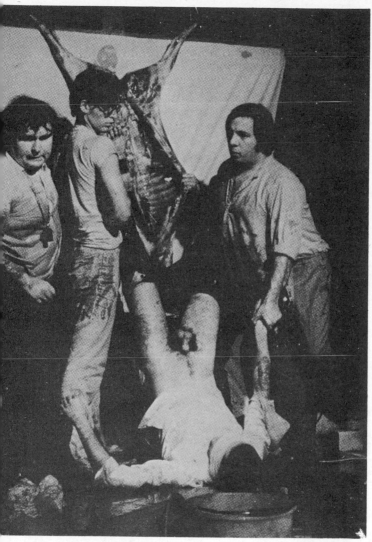

Hermann Nitsch (1938–   ). *Orgien-Mysterien-Theater*, January 1974. Action, Munich. Photo Kurt Benning.

57   In England Stuart Brisley is the only artist whose work has aspects in common with that of Beuys and with that of the Austrians. Brisley's speciality is the creation of disturbing and repellent 'life situations': performances in which the artist imprisons himself in filthy rooms bespattered with grey paint, or immerses himself in a bath full of rotting meat for a set number of hours each day. All his events are tightly structured in terms of duration, environment and meaning. Besides art galleries Brisley has performed at Hyde Park Corner, in car showrooms, on television and in a conventional theatre (he vomited on stage). His work, like that of Beuys, has radical political overtones: social criticism is implicit in all of it. The events cannot be marketed as art commodities in a capitalist system; they often take place outside art galleries in order to reach the general public. Brisley has also participated in the scheme for infiltrating artists into industry organized by the Artist Placement Group, and he has taken an active part in the foundation of the Artists' Union, a trade union for British artists.

Providing a complete contrast to the seriousness of Beuys and Brisley is the humorous vaudeville double-act of two London-based artists who have renounced the use of their surnames and have blended their separate identities into a composite 'living sculpture' known as Gilbert and George. Both artists studied sculpture at St Martin's in the mid-1960s, but ignored the Caro-inspired colour sculpture created by their predecessors. Their best-known performance, *Underneath the Arches* (1969–70), consisted of the artists standing on a table repeating a series of contrived movements like motorized statues, accompanied by a recording of the pre-war music-hall song which supplied the title of the piece. Apart from hands and faces covered with metallic paint, their clothes, accessories and hairstyles were outlandishly conservative.

In addition to performances of various kinds Gilbert and George have created a series of huge landscape paintings of themselves inspecting nature, mural-scale drawings of themselves in a shrubbery, videotapes of themselves getting tipsy on gin, photographs of themselves in various settings, and books and magazine articles recording their precious daily thoughts on art. Perversely, most of this disparate output is labelled 'sculpture'.

Like the superstars of the cinema or the idols of pop music, Gilbert and George have made their whole public lives into art. By dedicated self-promotion and careful attention to image, presentation and 'touch' they have become celebrities: 'We shall never cease to pose for you, Art.' They are famous for being famous. In return for their fame they offer their audiences wit, nostalgia, a parody of Englishness, and, above all, a devastating critique of the artistic life and the art world which they simultaneously send-up and milk.

As the convention of presenting art in the form of durable objects became discredited in the late 1960s, sculptors increasingly turned to their own bodies as subject matter and as a medium of expression. (Of course, dancers, mime artists, acrobats and strippers have exploited the language of the body for centuries.) The emergence of 'Body art' coincided with a widespread cultural interest in facial expression and in bodily gestures and attitudes, especially among psychologists.

For the sake of art Vito Acconci, Chris Burden, Terry Fox, Barry Le Va, Bruce Nauman, Dennis Oppenheim, Arnulf Rainer, Klaus Rinke, Keith Sonnier, William Wegman and others have subjected their bodies to a host of indignities. Parts of the body have been cast (by Nauman, for example, to illustrate the phrase 'from hand to mouth'); marks and incisions have been made on the skin; the flesh has been scorched by the sun (Oppenheim); hair has been burnt off, concrete blocks dropped on to toes, transformations of bodily processes and expressions produced by breathing exercises or by violent actions such as hurling the body against stone walls until exhausted (Le Va). Sexuality has not been ignored: *Seedbed* (1972), performed by Acconci in a New York gallery, consisted of the artist masturbating beneath a ramp. As Cindy Nemser remarks, there is 'a strain of sado-masochistic exhibitionism' in much Body art.

The activities of Performance and Body artists are inevitably transitory; and so documentation, in the form of interviews, photographs, films and video-tapes, is generated for the art market in large quantities.

The philosophical connection: Conceptual and Theoretical art

Since 1966 such a variety of artists and products have been categorized as 'Conceptual art' that the meaning of the term has become hopelessly diffuse. Originally, Conceptual art was a twofold enterprise concerned with (a) a theoretical examination of the concept 'art', and (b) putting forward concepts as art. The necessity for such an enterprise arose from the crisis in painting and the impasse of formalist and Minimal-ist aesthetics. The emergence of Conceptual art also reflected the iconoclastic *œuvre* of Marcel Duchamp, whose influence on avant-garde art since 1960 has exceeded that of any other artist. Three outstanding instances will give an idea of some of the issues involved.

An early work of the American artist Joseph Kosuth, *One and Three Chairs* (1965), presented the concept 'chair' by means of a real chair, a photograph of a chair and a dictionary definition of the word 'chair'. It illustrated the fact that physical form was not crucial to the presentation of concepts; in other words, Con-ceptual artists were not bound to create objects (unless one describes them as 'objects of thought') or to use traditional art media. In his later writings, Kosuth

Joseph Kosuth (1945–). *One and Three Chairs*, 1965.
Chair, photo of chair and dictionary definition.

argued that art was a 'language', that art works were
propositions 'presented within the context of art as
a comment on art', therefore each new artwork extended the existing concept of art. His statement 'art
is the definition of art' revealed that Kosuth believed
art to be a tautological system, or, as a nineteenth-
century theorist expressed it, 'art for art's sake'.

For a number of years Kosuth was associated with
the predominantly Anglo-American group of Conceptual artists known as Art and Language, whose
development is perhaps the most fascinating of any
in recent art. Other members of the group have
included Terry Atkinson, David Bainbridge, Michael
Baldwin, Ian Burn, Charles Harrison, Harold Hurrell,
Phillip Pilkington, Mel Ramsden and David Rushton,
but this list cannot be regarded as definitive because
the personnel of the group fluctuates continually.

In 1969, having concluded that the language of
words was the most suitable medium for investigating

63

the 'language' of art, Art and Language began to publish a journal; since then their utterances have been recorded on tape, on microfilm and on posters. Initially they adopted the methods of British analytical philosophy; later they ransacked a host of specialized disciplines in search of tools of thought. Generally they 'collage' their findings together, producing an almost incomprehensible (though often humorous) argot which infuriates the uninitiated.

Unfortunately the rational, academic disciplines proved of little value, and recently Art and Language have admitted that their investigation has become extremely problematical. The open-endedness of their search has led them into a no-man's-land outside existing subject fields, and now it has virtually ceased to have any connection with established forms of art, although their writings are still marketed in an art context. They continue to muse on the nature of their musing, and obsessively map and index their discourse in an attempt to uncover a structure or to discover a goal. A remark by Picasso, made in relation to painting, seems apposite: 'To search means nothing. . . . To find is the thing.'

An English artist who has been profoundly influenced by philosophy and logic, and one of the most trenchant critics of the Art and Language venture, is John Stezaker. Until recently his output consisted of essays systematically analysing the paradoxes of avant-garde art since Duchamp – especially those of Minimal and Conceptual art – and a series of 'art-statements' in various media which illustrate those paradoxes while simultaneously presenting an alternative logical basis for constructing artworks.

Stezaker's work is described as 'theoretical art' because in his search for a new synthesis of theory and practice the former is always given priority over the latter. Ends are given precedence over means, and the artist reverses the usual process of abstraction in art by working from the abstract to the particular.

Furthermore, Stezaker's approach is prescriptive rather than descriptive: he develops a theory *for* art not a theory *of* art; he is concerned with what art *ought* to be, not what it has been.

61   In 1973 Stezaker created *Mundus* ('world' or 'system'), consisting of an electronic apparatus displayed on a wall, plus a text entitled 'Beyond "art for art's sake"'. This ambitious work represents the first full articulation of his theories. The format of *Mundus* is that of a learning machine or game. It has a series of panels which can be illuminated in sequence by operating two control buttons; each panel contains a diagram divided into four different kinds of sign representing four concepts, Action, Custom, Learning and Law. The viewer plays the symbolic game by answering questions and by following one of two alternative pathways – subjective and objective – to reach a culminating point 'x' at the bottom of the machine.

In the words of its creator, *Mundus* is a 'functionalist artwork', whose purpose is not to represent external 'reality' but to prescribe a world of meanings to be apprehended by the intellect as the symbolic game is played. Furthermore, *Mundus* is an ideal type: it embodies ideal inter-relations within a microcosmic system; it proffers a function for art generally and at the same time embodies that function. *Mundus* deals with complex intellectual issues – fully described in Stezaker's text – and their articulation in physical terms satisfies two criteria of good science, and presumably also of good art: simplicity and elegance.

Mundus exemplifies a logical mode of art theory and practice which provides an alternative to the fatuity and paralysis typical of so much recent art. Stezaker's emphasis on the fact that art is a product of conscious human deliberation, and that artworks are primarily meanings or intentions, restores to the profession of artist a dignity that it was in great danger of forfeiting.

Chronology

1960   Greenberg's essay 'Modernist Painting' published in *Arts Yearbook,* New York.

1961   Groupe de Recherche d'Art Visuel (GRAV) founded in Paris. Manzoni's first *Living Sculptures.*

1962   Morris creates his first primary structures. Poons produces first discs on colour-field paintings.

1963   'Toward a New Abstraction', Jewish Museum, New York. Flavin's first tube lights.

1964   *Time* magazine discovers Op art. Shaped canvases at Guggenheim Museum, New York. 'Post-Painterly Abstraction', Los Angeles County Museum.

1965   Judd's essay 'Specific Objects' published in *Arts Yearbook.* 'New Generation' sculptors, Whitechapel Gallery, London. 'Washington Color Painters', Washington Gallery of Modern Art. 'The Responsive Eye', Museum of Modern Art, New York. Richard Wollheim's article 'Minimal Art' published in *Arts Magazine*, New York.

1966   'Primary Structures', Jewish Museum, New York. Destruction in Art Symposium (DIAS), London. 'Systemic painting', Guggenheim Museum, New York.

1967   'Art Povera', Genoa. Long's first cycling sculpture, Dibbets' first *Perspective Corrections.*

1968   Crumb's comic book *Zap* published. LeWitt writes 'Sentences on Conceptual Art'. 'Earthworks', Dwan Gallery, 'Anti-Form', John Gibson Gallery, New York. 'Minimal Art', Gemeentemuseum, The Hague. 'Serial Imagery', Pasadena. 'Art of the Real', New York, Paris.

1969   First issue of *Art-Language* published. 'Ecologic Art', John Gibson Gallery, New York. 'When Attitudes Become Form', Berne, Amsterdam and London. 'Konzeption /Conception', Städtisches Museum, Leverkusen. 'Op Losse Schroeven', Stedelijk Museum, Amsterdam.

1970   Supports/Surfaces group, Paris. 'Happening and Fluxus', Kunstverein, Cologne. 'Conceptual Art and Conceptual Aspects', New York Cultural Center. 'Information', Museum of Modern Art, 'Software', Jewish Museum, New York.

1971   'Artist Placement Group', Hayward Gallery, London. Hyper-Realism, at 7th Paris Biennale. 'Art and Technology', Los Angeles County Museum. 'Robert Morris', Tate Gallery, London. Haacke's Guggenheim show cancelled.

1972   'Sharp-Focus Realism', Sidney Janis Gallery, New

York. 'Grids', University of Pennsylvania. 'Documents 5', Kassel, on the theme of questioning reality. 'The New Art', Hayward Gallery, and 'The Avant-garde in Britain', Gallery House, London.

1973 'Prospect 73', Düsseldorf, devoted to Minimal painting. Stezaker's *Mundus*, Nigel Greenwood Gallery, London. 1974 'Contemporanea', Rome. 'Yves Klein and Piero Manzoni', Tate Gallery, London.

Further Reading

Catalogues, articles, monographs and books on particular movements can be traced via art bibliographies such as *Art Index* and *Art Design Photo*. Several anthologies of articles are available in paperback : for example, *The New Art* (1966), *Minimal Art* (1968), *Idea Art* (1973), all edited by Gregory Battcock and published in New York by Dutton. Also available are selections of articles and reviews by major American critics: Harold Rosenberg, *The De-definition of Art* (New York, 1972) and *Discovering the Present* (Chicago, 1973); Lucy R. Lippard, *Changing* (New York, 1971); N. and E. Calas, *Icons and Images of the Sixties* (New York, 1971), Max Kozloff, *Renderings* (New York and London, 1970).

Two generously illustrated books on American art are Henry Geldzahler's *New York Painting and Sculpture: 1940–1970* (New York and London, 1969) and Sam Hunter's *American Art of the 20th Century* (New York and London, 1973); and on French art Jean Clair's *L'Art en France, une nouvelle génération* (Paris, 1973).

Those interested in the link between science, technology and art should read Jonathan Benthall's *Science and Technology in Art Today* (London and New York, 1972), Douglas Davis's *Art and the Future* (New York and London, 1973) and Jack Burnham's *Beyond Modern Sculpture* (New York and London, 1968). Other aspects of art since 1966 are described in Germano Celant's *Art Povera* (London and New York, 1969), G. Muller's *The New Avant-garde* (New York and London, 1972), U. Meyer's *Conceptual Art* (New York 1972) and Lucy R. Lippard's *Six Years* (New York and London, 1973); a more theoretical approach is adopted by Jack Burnham in *The Structure of Art* (New York, 1971). Finally, definitions of movements, groups and styles are given in my book *A Glossary of Art, Architecture and Design Since 1945* (London, 1973.)

List of Illustrations

Measurements are given in inches and centimetres, height first. Where one measurement exceeds 240 in, feet and metres are used.

12   Kenneth Noland (1924–). *Via Token*, 1969. Acrylic emulsion on canvas, 100 × 240 (253.1 × 610). Courtesy André Emmerich Gallery, New York. See p. 8.

13   Kenneth Noland (1924–). *Up Cadmium*, 1966. Acrylic on canvas, 72 × 216 (183 × 549). Courtesy André Emmerich Gallery, New York. See p. 8.

14   Larry Poons (1937–). *Untitled-2*, 1970. Acrylic on canvas, 89 × 113½ (226 × 339). See p. 14.

15   Larry Poons (1937–). *Knoxville*, 1966. Acrylic on canvas, 118 × 157½ (300 × 400). Private collection. See p. 14.

16   Larry Poons (1937–). *No. 5*, 1972. Acrylic on canvas, 103½ × 74 (263 × 188). Courtesy of Knoedler Contemporary Art, Lawrence Rubin, Director, New York. See p. 14.

17   Bridget Riley (1931–). *Disturbance*, 1964. Emulsion on canvas, 68 × 68 (173 × 173). Courtesy of the artist. See p. 13.

18   Bridget Riley (1931–). *Study for Chant I*, 1967. Gouache on paper, 40 × 27 (101.6 × 68.6). Courtesy of the artist. See p. 13.

19   Dan Flavin (1933–). *untitled (to Alexandra)*, 1973. Pink fluorescent lights, paired 48 in. (122 cm) fixtures placed vertically at 24 in. (61 cm) intervals with four rows of 24 in. (61 cm) fixtures at 14 in. (35.5 cm) intervals horizontally between them. Courtesy of the artist. See p. 30.

20   Dan Flavin (1933–). *untitled (to SM)*, 1969. Red, yellow, pink and blue fluorescent lights, 9 ft 6 in × 8 ft × 64 ft 1 in. (2.89 × 2.44 × 19.54 m). Courtesy of the artist. See p. 30.

21   Larry Bell (b. 1939). *Untitled*, 1969–70. Coated glass, ⅜ × 120 × 6 (1 × 345 × 15.2). Courtesy of the Pace Gallery, New York. See pp. 24, 30.

22   Robert Morris (1939–). *Hearing*, 1972. Copper chair, lead bed, galvanized aluminium table, platform 144 (367) square. See p. 33.

23   John McCracken (1934–). *There's No Reason Not To*, 1967. Wood and fibreglass, 120 × 8 × 3½ (305 × 20.3 × 8.9). Nicholas Wilder Gallery, Los Angeles. See p. 19.

24 Donald Judd (1928–). *Untitled,* 1968. Galvanized iron and aluminium, $9 \times 40 \times 31$ ($23 \times 102 \times 79$). Los Angeles County Museum of Art. See pp. 19, 26.

25 Barry Flanagan (1941–). *Three Sculptures,* 1967: *4 casb 2'67,* sand and canvas; *ringl 1'67,* linoleum; *rope (gr 2sp60) 6'67,* sisal. Courtesy of Rowan Gallery Ltd. See p. 17.

26 Carl Andre (1935–). *Scatterpiece,* 1967. Photo courtesy of Weber Gallery, New York. See p. 17.

27 Phillip King (1934–). *Blue Between,* 1971. Painted steel, $87 \times 180 \times 144$ ($221 \times 458 \times 356$). Courtesy of Rowan Gallery Ltd. See p. 21.

28 Phillip King (1934–). *Through,* 1965. Fibreglass, $84 \times 108 \times 132$ ($213 \times 274 \times 335$). Richard L. Feigen & Co., Inc., New York. See p. 21.

29 William Turnbull (1922–). *Sculpture,* 1969–70. Three wooden frames, each $1\frac{3}{4} \times 59\frac{1}{4} \times 59\frac{1}{4}$ ($4.5 \times 150.5 \times 150.5$). Courtesy of the artist. See p. 23.

30 Richard Smith (1931–). *Clairol Wall,* 1967. Acrylic on canvas, $8 \times 32 \times 3$ ft ($2.43 \times 9.76 \times 0.91$ m). Courtesy of Galerie Denise René-Hans Mayer, Krefeld. See p. 16.

31 Richard Smith (1931–). *Gift Wrap,* 1963. Oil on canvas, $80 \times 208 \times 33$ ($203 \times 528 \times 84$). Courtesy of Kasmin Ltd. See p. 16.

32 Richard Smith (1931–). *White Rope,* 1973. Acrylic on canvas, aluminium rod and various strings, 103×48 (261×122). Courtesy of Kasmin Ltd, photo Garage Art Ltd. See p. 18.

33 Anthony Caro (1921–). *Straight Flush,* 1972. Painted steel, $78 \times 145 \times 52$ ($198 \times 368 \times 132$). Courtesy of Kasmin Ltd. See p. 20.

34 William Tucker (1935–). *Beulah I,* 1971. Steel piping, $60\frac{1}{4} \times 106$ (153×269). Photo courtesy of Kasmin Ltd. See p. 22.

35 Ron Davis (1937–). *Untitled,* 1968. Fibreglass, 60×144 (152×366). Ludwig Collection, Wallraf-Richardtz Museum, Cologne. See p. 47.

36 Tom Phillips (1937–). *Berlin Wall with German Grass and Skies,* 1973. Acrylic on canvas, 60×84 (152×213). Marlborough Fine Arts (London) Ltd. See p. 46.

37 Mark Lancaster (1938–). *Cambridge Michaelmas*, 1969. Liquitex on canvas, 68 × 68 (172.8 × 172.8). Charles Gordon, London, See p. 47.

38 Shusaku Arakawa (1936–). *10 Reassembling,* 1968–69. Oil, pencil and magic marker on canvas. Collection of the artist. See p. 49.

39 Sol LeWitt (1923–). *Four Basic Colours,* 1971. Print, $7\frac{7}{8} \times 10$ (20 × 25.4). Lisson Gallery, by courtesy of the artist. See p. 30.

40 Robert Smithson (1938–73). *Spiral Jetty*, 1970. Diameter 160 ft (49 m). Great Salt Lake, Utah. See p. 35.

41 Robert Morris (1931–). *Observatory*, 1971. Earth mound, diameter 230 ft (70m). Ijmuiden, photo courtesy of the Leo Castelli Gallery. See pp. 33, 35.

42 Michael Heizer (1944–). *Double Negative*, 1969–70. Excavation, 29 × 49 × 1480 ft (9 × 15 × 450 m). Mormon Mesa, Nevada, photo collection Virginia Dwan. See p. 35.

43 Hans Haacke (1936–). *Floating Ice Ring*, 1970–71. See p. 39.

44 Eva Hesse (1936–70). *Untitled (7 Poles)*, 1970. Fibreglass over polyethylene, tallest pole 111 (282.1). Photo Paulus Leeser. See p. 32.

45 Jan Dibbets (1941–). *Dutch Mountain – Big Sea*, 1971. Eleven colour photographs on aluminium, $179 \times 33\frac{7}{8}$ (758 × 84.8). The Museum of Modern Art, New York. See p. 38.

46 Dennis Oppenheim (1938–). *Reading Position*, 1970. Two photographs. Courtesy Sonnabend Gallery, New York, Paris. See p. 53.

47 Malcolm Morley (1931–). *Race Track*, 1970. Acrylic on canvas, 69 × 87 (175 × 220). Ludwig Collection, Neue Galerie, Aachen. See p. 44.

48 Robert Cottingham (1935–). *Roxy*, 1971–72. Oil on canvas, 78 × 78 (198 × 198). Collection Mr Saul P. Steinberg, New York. See pp. 43, 44.

49 David Hockney (1937–). *Early Morning, St Maxence*, 1968. Acrylic on canvas, 48 × 60 (122 × 153). Private collection. See p. 43.

50 Duane Hanson (1925–). *Tourists*, 1970. Fibreglass and polychromed polyester, 64 × 65 × 47 (162.7 × 165 × 119.3). Collection Mr Saul P. Steinberg, New York. See pp. 44–45.

51 Chuck Close (1940–). *Kent*, 1971. Coloured drawing, $24\frac{3}{4} \times 21\frac{5}{8}$ (63×55). Collection Mme Deloffre, Paris. Photo Galerie de Gestlo, Hamburg. See pp. 43, 44.

52 Claudio Bravo (1936–). *Portrait of Antonio Cores,* 1973. Oil on canvas, 79×59 (200×150). Sara Hilden Collection, Art Museum of the Ateneum, Helsinki. Photo courtesy of Staempfli Gallery, New York. See p. 43.

53 Mark Boyle (1934–) and Joan Hills (–). *Liquid Light Environment*, 1966–67. Photo by John Claxton. See p. 41.

54 Martin Sharp. *Vincent van Gogh Poster*. $28\frac{1}{2} \times 19\frac{1}{4}$ (72.5×48.8). See p. 41.

55 Alan Shields (1944–). *Devil Devil, Love*, 1970. Mixed media, 96×196 (244×498). Paula Cooper Gallery. See p. 42.

56 John Walker (1939–). *Sometime II*, 1971. 96×240 (244×610). Collection Frank Porter, courtesy of Paula Cooper Gallery, New York. See p. 43.

57 Stuart Brisley (1933–). *Artist as Whore; an Event*, Christmas 1971–72. Action, Gallery House, London, courtesy of the artist. See p. 52.

58 Günter Brus (1938–). *Test to Destruction*, 1970. Action, Munich. Courtesy of the artist. See p. 50.

59 Gilbert and George (both 1942–). *Morning Light on Art for All*, Spring 1972. Colour photograph. Nigel Greenwood Inc. Ltd, courtesy of Art for All. See p. 53.

60 Joseph Beuys (1921–). *Scene from the Deer Hunt*, 1961. Assemblage, app. $72 \times 60 \times 24$ ($183 \times 153 \times 61$). Photo courtesy Stedelijk Van Abbemuseum, Eindhoven. See p. 49.

61 John Stezaker (1945–). *Mundus*, 1973. Perspex and wood, $59 \times 17\frac{1}{8} \times 3150$ 43.5×7.5). Nigel Greenwood Inc. Ltd. See p. 57.

62 Bruce Nauman (1941–). *From Hand to Mouth*, 1967. Wax over cloth, $30 \times 10 \times 4$ ($76.2 \times 25.4 \times 10.1$). Private Collection. See p. 53.

63 Art and Language. *Poster Statement from the Series 'Them and Us'*, 1973. Poster, 22×18 (55.8×45.7). Collection of Paul Maentz, Cologne. Photo Lisson Gallery, courtesy of Terry Atkinson. See p. 55.

1

2

7

8

9

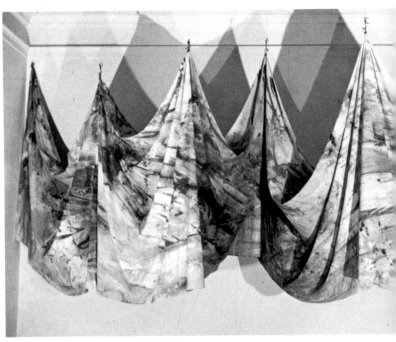

10

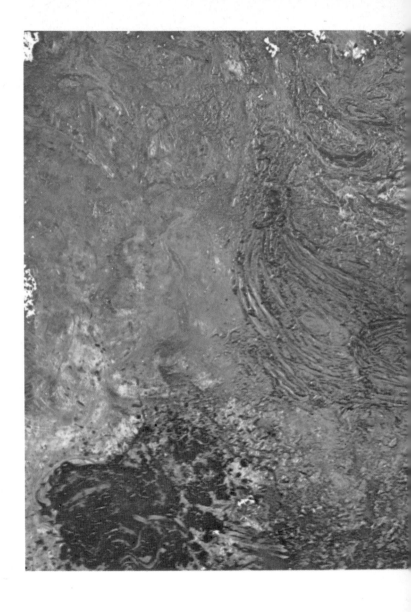

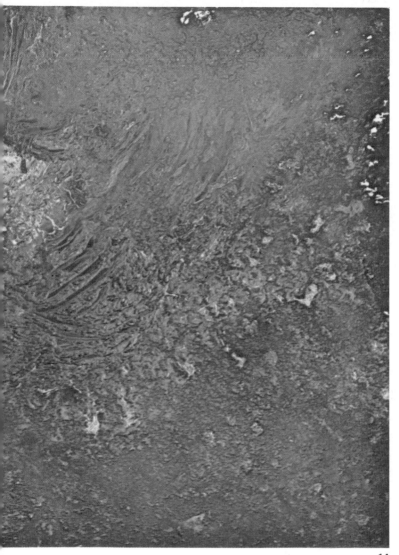

14

15

17

19

21

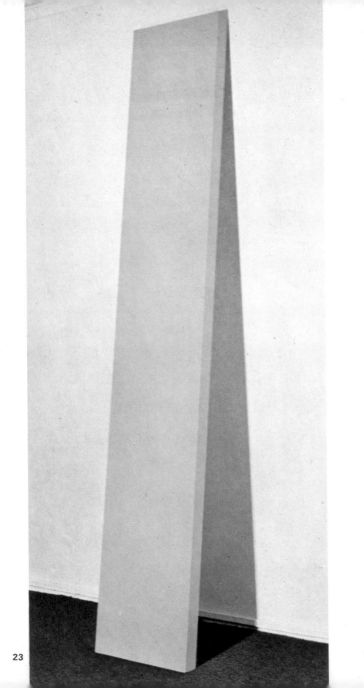

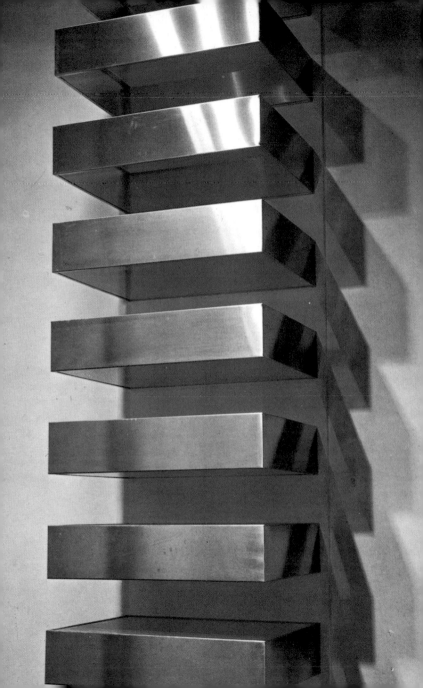

25

26 ▶

27

28

31

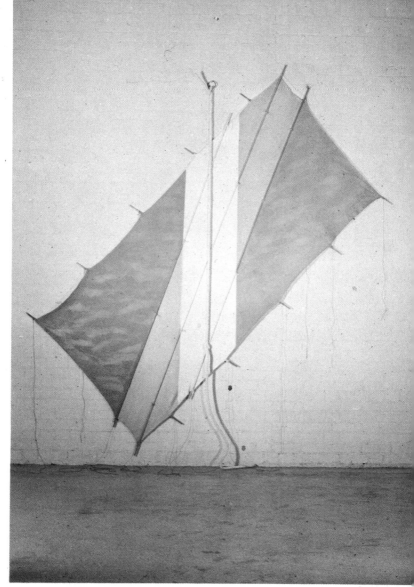

33

35

37

AN INVESTIGATION OF THE ELEMENTS OF REASSEMBLY AND OF THE POSSIBLE APPLICATIONS OF THESE IN ORDER TO CHANGE USAGE

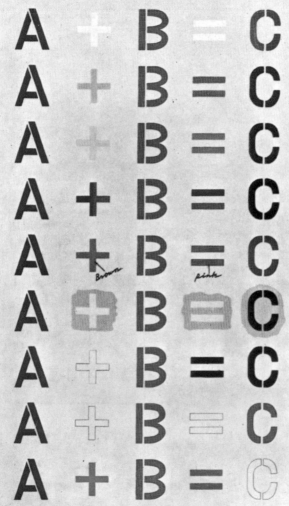

A + B = C

TO WHAT EXTENT IS = A FUNCTION OF + ?

The range of values for each + and = is wide open as long as the above relations hold.
Other considerations are: A + + + + + B = C   A + B ——————— C
Color, positional changes in A, B
If + is ten years (minutes) ahead of =
Or a shift in any other dimension——

38

Yellow

Black

Yellow/Black

Yellow/Red

Black/Blue

Red/Blue

Yellow/Red/Blue

Black/Red/Blue

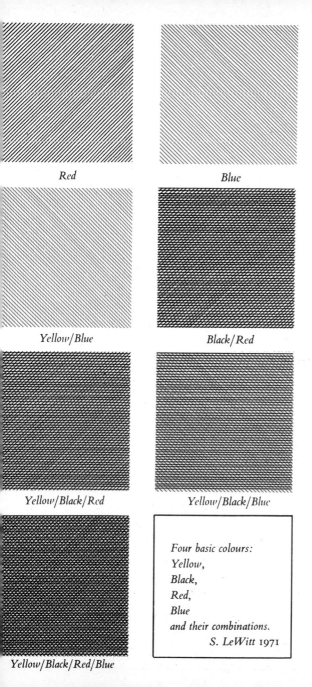

Red

Blue

Yellow/Blue

Black/Red

Yellow/Black/Red

Yellow/Black/Blue

Yellow/Black/Red/Blue

Four basic colours:
Yellow,
Black,
Red,
Blue
and their combinations.
S. LeWitt 1971

40

41

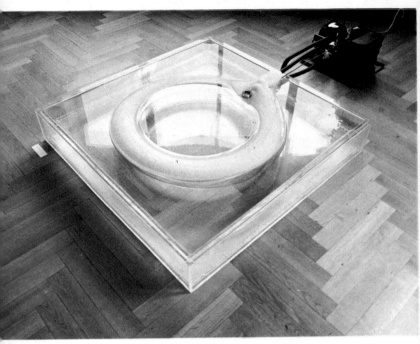

43

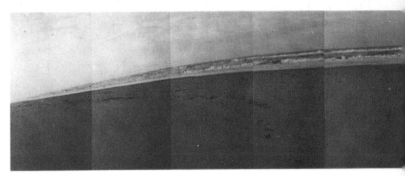

45

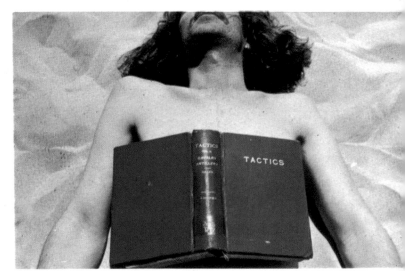

46

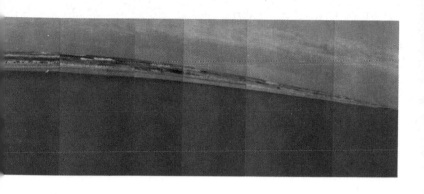

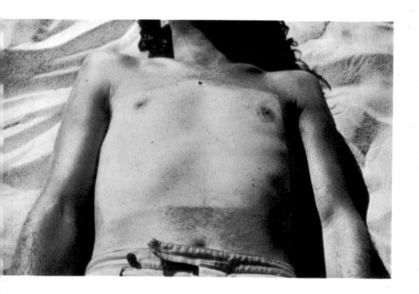

south africa

Greyville Race Course—Durban, South Africa

48

49

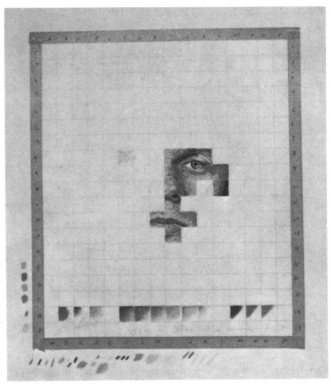

51

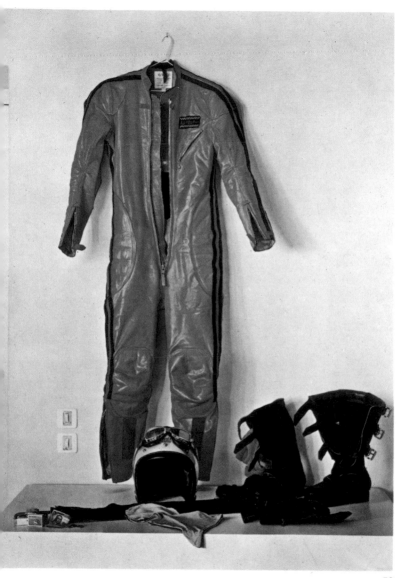

52

53, 54 ▶

i have a terrible lucidity at moments, when nature is so glorious in those days I am hardly conscious of myself and the picture comes to me like in a dream...

vincent

55

56

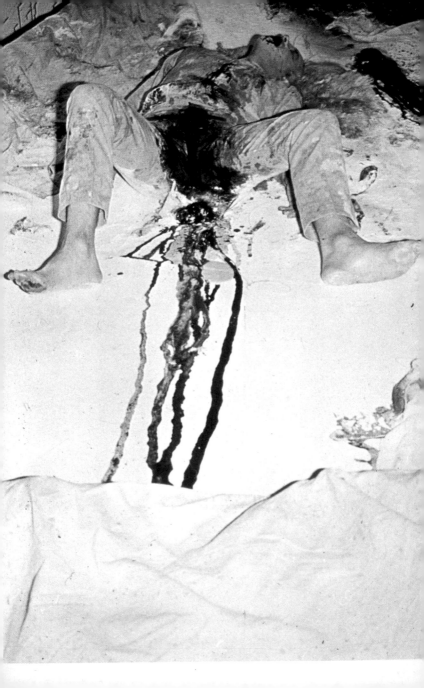

58

61

62 ▶

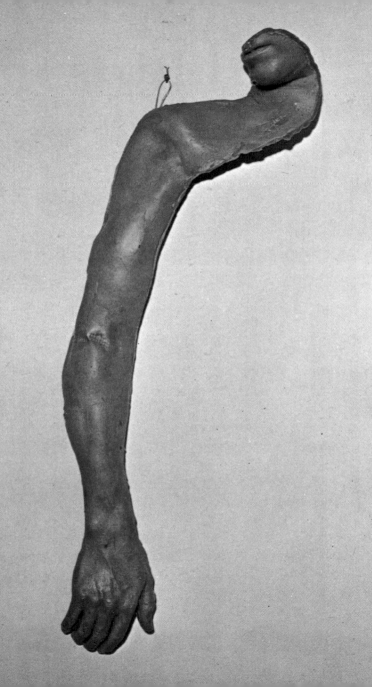

(1) It seems fairly obvious that the traditional methodological 'style' inculcates the view that separate inquiries (activities) are essentially sui generis. This instantiates a worthless (or at least very limited) psychological model of inquiry: so-called inquiry (in 'art' or in the community art) remains a bastion of uncritical methodological egocentricity. Perhaps this is why phenomenologists always took art so seriously.

(2) There is no suggestion that what is advocated is an encyclopedic 'unity', or unification. The requirements of soundness (of concepts used) and adequacy are not all positivistic.

The dimension of the institute which involves ideology - critique - involves paradigm change, i.e., the entertainment of the prospect of it.

And whilst 'Art-Language' (the journal of the institute) is the 'normal' publication, it will do nothing to support the simplistic encyclopedia charge.

(3) In accord with this, the textbook is to be regarded as open-ended: recursive and adaptive. The production of the textbook is 'depth' institute activity. Its information status, or 'informativeness analysis', may give a different notion of information than that appropriate to the journal.

(4) We have sustained a lot of criticism (some sensitive, some hysterical) that the language(s) we use, are interested in, are hard to understand, inconsistent, etc. It seems odd that the prospect of linguistic specialization at some stage should remain open. The point is that our languages are neither (all) necessarily 'thin' (bearing a relation of minimum proportion to 'thick' ones) or necessarily 'thick'. Considering the proportionality may be important as interpretive exercise.

(5) The examination of the interface between 'conception', whatever it is, and 'perception', whatever it is, is basic to most institute discourse. Another prospect of ideology critique (without psychoanaltyic credulity) is to be located in relation to this interface. There is a need to consider the problems in hermeneutic method. This is interconnected with the conception/perception problem. And trying to talk to each other is of obvious importance.